Hoop Dreams Fulfilled:
An Athlete's Failures and Redemption on His Journey to Professional Basketball

Tyson Hartnett

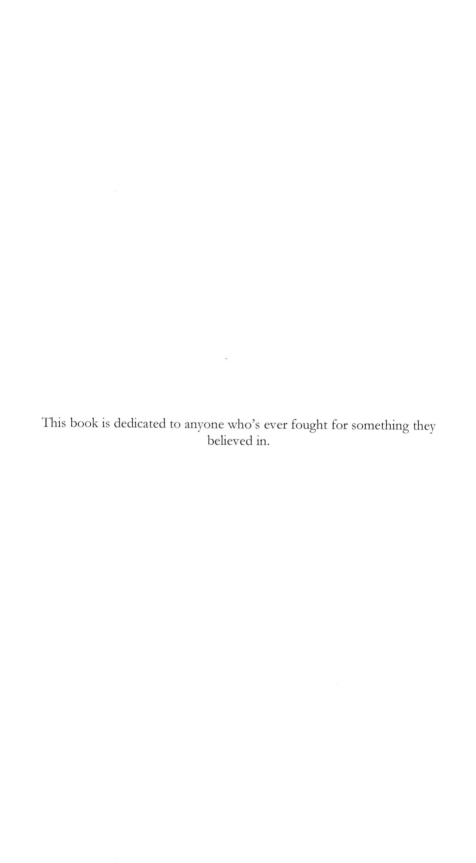

This book is dedicated to anyone who's ever fought for something they believed in.

CONTENTS

Author's note: Some names have been changed.

ACKNOWLEDGMENTS

First off, I'd like to thank my editor Brian Clark Howard for perfecting the prose and helping me tell this story. I'm eternally grateful to him for making me realize that not everybody knows what an agility ladder is or what AAU stands for.

Another thanks to Rick Robinson, Trevor Carrozza, Ivan Klochko, Jason Grad, and Jozef Durkáč for helping with the cover photo and artistic design.

I want to thank the guys I grew up playing basketball with who opened my eyes to the sport: Coach Derek Satchell, Coach Joel Ettinger, Jared Ettinger, Matt Sosna, Kofi Dwebeng, Kraig Peters, Jason Thompson, Dave Torres, Vinny Ciecka, and Brad Cohen. Also, I want to thank Mike Scarduzio, James Marion, Craig Wager, Ryan "Big Man" Blasczyk, Gil Sanchez, and Kyle Santoferraro for being there for me when I wasn't the most outgoing kid. Also, Kevin Atwell for pushing me to stay disciplined at an early age.

I want to thank Chris Bruff, Jon Sheets, Phil Bofia, Dominique Scales, Kevin Reed, Olli, Junior Bernal, Ammar, Ernie, Fresh, and Jesse Keith for busting my ass day after day in my first year of Division 1 basketball.

Also, Aaron Spellman, Kevin Darby, Billy Care, Tim Matchett, Sean Hughes, Mike Cilento, and all the guys on the Rowan Basketball team. You guys brought me in and treated me like family, so for that I'm extremely grateful.

In Sweden, I want to thank Anton for being a good friend, Freddy, Ulf, James, Coach Mats, Anna, and the rest of the Nassjo community who showed me love.

In Argentina, I want to thank Tuti, Luis, Nico, Manu, and all the guys on Tiro Federal for being such great teammates with me. Pablo, you were a life-saver when I initially got to Cordoba so I'm forever in your debt. Also, coaches Jose Pettuggia and Damien. And Donald Jones for helping me out big time with getting onto the different teams. I also want to thank everybody on my team in Chile.

I'd also like to thank Coach Mike Burden, Dr. John Gianinni, Joe Cassidy, and Dave Lafferty for being great coaches and leaders in my life. Also, big

i

thank you to Bobbito Garcia aka Kool Bob Love for bringing me in and letting me play in all your open runs and tournaments.

Rick, no words can express how much I appreciate all you have helped me with throughout my life. Your tactics were unusual but deep down I know you always had the best intentions not only for me, but for every athlete you ever coached. Coaching young, cocky ballplayers is tough, but you make it work year after year. I honestly have no idea how you do it.

I want to thank everybody in my family, and specifically Uncle Mike, Aunt Sue, Uncle John, Aunt Gigi, Grandma, Aunt Shauna and Uncle Roger for helping me out when things weren't perfect in my life. You were all there for me when I needed it so I have no words to express my gratitude.

Thanks to my sister, Ali Hartnett, for dealing with me growing up, helping out with photos, and just being a great sister overall. I finally think you're ready for 'Nam.

Finally, I'd like to thank my Mom and Dad for being there with me throughout this journey. I know I wasn't the easiest person to deal with growing up, so I thank you for not losing hope in me, especially in the hard times.

Prologue

One of the scariest things in life is thinking that you're not making any progress. You put in the work, but you don't believe you're getting anywhere. You have visions for the future but at the time it seems like nothing is happening.

The following words you're about to read are about trust. Trust in oneself, but also trust in that higher power. Whether it's God, the universe, or just plain luck, there's got to be something out there pulling us and directing our steps. If not, I've got no explanation for the stories in this book.

I've been pulled to basketball from an early age and couldn't do anything about it. I fell in love with the game and the training, even if I wasn't that great of a player at times. But I trusted that the more work I put in, the better I'd become.

This story is about my path to professional basketball, but it's also about the lessons I learned along the way. It's about the real-life events that occur if you're not careful, or if you neglect certain areas of your life. Being an athlete with my only mission to play in the NBA, I neglected too many other aspects of my life.

Breaking it down, life is simple. If we work hard and stay honest, good things happen. If we get lazy and neglect areas of our life, bad things happen. Obviously we can't control every external thing along the way, but we can control our attitude and decide if we'll keep moving forward.

It was scary writing this book, knowing that whoever reads it will know my deepest, darkest secrets. But at the end of the day, we all go through similar scenarios. We're all trying to hide things. I'm not the first and I won't be the last. But maybe, instead of hiding, how about we bring it to light?

Maybe someone who reads these words will be able to get through their situation a little easier. And for that, it'll all be worth it.

My only goal growing up was to make the NBA. I wanted a fairy tale life of receiving a Division 1 scholarship, playing at that school for four years to get my college degree, then playing in the NBA until my retirement. I thought that's what would happen if I worked hard enough.

Reality, though, turned out to be much different.

1
A SEED IS PLANTED

One day during one of the lowest points of my life, I stepped outside, picked up a basketball, and started dribbling again. I hadn't touched a ball in months, but I was immediately transported back to my freshman year of high school, when I would spend hours shooting in the cold, trying to get as many minutes as I could on the JV team. I thought about how life took some weird turns, but at that moment the smell and feeling of the ball in my hands felt so good.

I kept dribbling, eventually walking out to the street in front of the house. For over an hour, I did the same dribbling drills I performed years earlier, mixing in different moves like there was someone playing defense on me. My handle was horrible, but after every dribble I felt myself getting it back ever so slightly. When I finished dribbling, I shot for a few minutes in the driveway. It felt amazing, and I wondered why I had given this up in the first place.

Following my psychiatrist's advice, I tried to exercise as much as possible in those days. It gave me a sense of power after every session, also providing me with clarity of what I wanted to do in the future.

Shortly after that, an old friend who still lived in the area pushed me to play with him at some courts nearby. I told him I was rusty and out of shape, but he kept asking me. Eventually I gave in and went with him. Being around the guys and playing again felt amazing. It was the same trash talking I grew up with, and I actually still had game. I wasn't scoring every play but the talent was there. I knew, and felt in my bones, that there was potential.

Despite everything that had happened, I realized, *Things are good when I play basketball.* The sport was sneaking its way back into my life, but I knew the dangers of overdoing it. I told myself to take it slow.

\--

Long before those days, my basketball career started in fourth grade.

My first real memories of the game were in Atco, New Jersey, playing on an older team. I passed the ball every time I got it. I wasn't very good, but just being on the court with the fifth and sixth graders got me accustomed to the game.

At my elementary school, I played with an older janitor in the gym when classes finished. At first I wasn't good, but I practiced with him so much that I eventually began to hit long-distance shots.

In Atco, we also had a basketball hoop outside my family's house. When the older guys in the neighborhood came by to play, they were amazed how good I was for only being in elementary school. Playing HORSE, I beat them nearly every time. When I had nobody to play with, I'd call friends who didn't play basketball and say, "If you come play one on one against me, I'll give you money when I make the NBA." They were an easy match, but it was nice to play against someone instead of just shooting by myself for hours.

For a while growing up in middle school, I bullied a kid who lived down the street from me named James. Nearly every day, I'd say to him, "Can I beat you up?"

One day, he had enough and started hitting me. I walked home crying and when my mom saw me, she asked what happened. I said behind tears, "James beat me up."

She dragged me over to his house. When we got there, James said, "Look, he bullies me every day saying, 'Can I beat you up?' I just got sick of it and retaliated." I felt like an idiot. After that, I never picked on him again.

In fact, I tried never to pick on anyone else again. I learned to try to stay humble and treat people the way I wanted to be treated.

From an early age, I developed strong determination and persistence. In fifth grade, my friend Kevin could spin the ball on his finger. It was something flashy he could do that I couldn't do at the time... and it pissed me off. I believed I was a better player, but he had better ball handling skills that could entertain people. I got so annoyed by this that I was determined to spin the ball on my finger.

For hours every day, I practiced and practiced. Finally, after about a month, I did it. I could consistently spin the ball on my finger while tapping it lightly to keep it going. To this day I still have that skill, learned after one month of practice in fifth grade.

On the court, Kevin was my basketball buddy. I didn't have an older brother so he was the one who pushed me. We both took basketball seriously. We used to play two on ten during recess in elementary school. There were limited hoops and only two balls, so we approached everybody on the court and said, "We'll play you all, two on ten." They often agreed, at first snickering, but Kevin and I proceeded to win almost every time. He'd throw the ball to the hoop and I'd somehow catch it between all the defenders and make the layup.

In his backyard, Kevin had a slab of concrete with a hoop. On the weekends, we'd play one on one for hours. He would win some, I would win some, but we battled all day long. We lived by military-style sayings like, "pain is weakness leaving the body," pushing ourselves to see how long we could go without water during the hot summer days. We never made excuses or complained. One of his best lines was, "It's not what kind of shoes you're wearing, it's what's in the shoes that matters." *(Editor's note: After college, Kevin became a lieutenant in the U.S. Army.)*

In sixth grade, I kept busy playing basketball, baseball, and soccer. I was a solid pitcher and an excellent goalie. However, I had to make a choice. I liked playing all three sports, but I couldn't do them all full-time because the seasons overlapped.

There are moments in life when subtle signs can direct you on which way to go. If you're not open and aware, you will miss them. One of these signs was when our family went to Mexico for a surfing trip. When we got to the hotel, there was a half-court outdoor basketball area right below our room. In our whole time in Mexico, I don't think I saw another basketball hoop, besides the one right where we stayed. I took that as a sign I should continue to play basketball.

Another reason I stopped playing baseball is because of the Scott Heebner fastball. Scott Heebner was a player in my league who pitched the ball very fast, but a bit out of control. When I got up to the plate to bat, I often got hit by pitches and I was worried he might hit me in the face, seriously injuring me. That's not something I wanted to deal with, so if you're reading this Scott, thanks for helping me make my decision towards basketball.

When I made my decision, I knew that if I was going to take basketball seriously, I'd have to take training seriously. Since I had no idea how to train other than running around the courts with the ball, I started to do some research on basketball drills. At the time, the internet was a new thing. There was no YouTube and cell phones didn't exist. I did a search on my AOL dial-up connection for basketball drills, finding a page of two-ball dribbling exercises that somebody had created. I printed out that page and for the next six years, those formed the core of my ball-handling workouts.

Eventually, I learned more complex drills at the basketball camps I went to in the summers. After sixth grade, Kevin and I attended the Shawnee Renegade Basketball Camp in Medford, a town twenty minutes away from Atco. Shawnee was a powerhouse school, consistently ranked in the top ten in the state. Every summer for four weeks, they had a basketball camp for kids in middle school. We learned ball handling, shooting, defense, and conditioning drills. I looked up to the instructors and listened to them when they told us that these drills were worthless unless we did them every day.

After school, I did the drills out in the street, creating little games and workout plans. I tried to remember as much as I could from the camp, playing outside for hours every day. Sometimes guys from the neighborhood would stop by for a game.

The night before a school game in sixth grade, I ran around the blacktop for hours under the cool night sky. After the game the following night, my friend Craig, who was doing the scorebook, came up to me. Excited, he said, "Tyson, you had 39 points!"

I looked at the score sheet, which was messy, full of twos and ones. There was a 39 in my column. I thought about how much I had trained the night before and how a day later I scored 39 points. That planted the seed in my mind that if I just worked hard, good things would happen.

Because playing by myself all day was only going to get me so far, I got onto a travel team with a few players from the area. The coach was an ex-football player, so all the practices were intense. For some reason I often got injured, whether it was getting my nose busted or elbowed pretty bad.

One of my teammates was a player named Kofi. At the time, he was destined to be the next Michael Jordan. He was only about five feet tall, but he scored nearly every possession and had amazing ball-handling skills for being so young. One game he made a ridiculous dribbling move through three defenders and made a layup. My dad was sitting across from me in the bleachers and we locked eyes with an expression that said, "Holy crap, did you just see that?"

Another constant during this time was the Saturday morning workouts by former professional basketball player Rick Barrett. Standing 6'10" tall and about 45 years old, Rick at first appears intimidating to nearly everyone. He had played pro in Argentina when he got out of college, but since then he had been coaching a travel team every summer called the Gym Rats. Each year, they'd go to tournaments all over the country in Vegas, Los Angeles, Baltimore, and anywhere else the scouts would be. He's very well-connected and knows coaches, agents, and players all across the world.

During these workouts, about a hundred of the best young athletes from South Jersey arrived at a middle school gym in Voorhees, New Jersey. For the first hour, we did drills. In the second hour, we played games with the winners staying on the court. Being ten years old and playing against the best players in South Jersey was an eye-opener, making me realize I wasn't nearly as good as I thought I was.

Going into seventh grade, the school district was set up so that kids in Atco attended Edgewood High School in Winslow. Winslow was primarily African-American, and it was the first time I was a minority. Other guys from my neighborhood were nervous, thinking that we'd get targeted and bullied every day.

For the first few days at Edgewood, I *was* nervous. However, I realized it wasn't nearly as different as I had thought. There were daily fights in the hallways but nobody specifically bullied me just to do it. I once had a Snapple stolen from my locker but that was the worst of it.

This was still a new school and, unfortunately for me, I wasn't that good at making friends. I wasn't a loser but I felt like one at times. At lunch, I sat at a table all by myself or with one other kid who I barely knew. Right behind me was a table with a bunch of girls and guys that I knew, but for some reason I thought they were too cool to sit with. Even though they knew me, none of them invited me to sit with them. Once in a while at lunch a third kid sat with us named Jerry, but he was always suspended for weeks on end. I don't even remember what the kid's name was who I sat with. We talked about video games once in a while, but for the most part we were just happy not to be sitting completely alone.

I felt like a loser, but when the basketball season started everything changed. When tryouts came, Kevin and I were two of the best players. We were the only white guys on the team. Most of the other players were more athletic and stronger than us although Kevin and I worked out as much as we could. On road trips it was definitely a culture shock being two of the only white guys on the entire bus. At first I was nervous about that but when we proved we could play ball, it didn't matter if we were black, white, blue, or yellow, we had game and that's all that mattered.

On school nights, I'd retire to the basement of our house to do a vertical jump program I bought off the internet. For about an hour every night, I listened to DMX, barking while performing the jumping exercises. When my younger sister was peacefully eating dinner, I'd be barking at her while doing calf raises on the steps to the kitchen.

One of the proudest moments for me that year came when we were walking though the gym on the way to the bus for an away game. An older, cooler kid I'd seen around school was in a gym class. He pointed at me and said, "Yea, you're going to play good today." I'd never spoken to him before, but it felt good to get some recognition from an older kid just because I played basketball.

In eighth grade, things started to shift. In order to have a better chance of continuing my basketball career, I couldn't keep going to Edgewood. Rick Barrett told my parents that if I had any shot of playing in college, I'd have to attend a bigger, more competitive school. The team at Edgewood was decent but college coaches never attended.

On my travel team at the time, I wasn't even that good of a player. I did well at Edgewood but once it came to higher competition, I couldn't hang. I rarely scored and was slow compared to everybody else. Going to tournaments and seeing the level of competition, I knew something had to be done.

A loophole in the system that many athletes take advantage of is staying back in their grade for a year. My grades were great, but if I wanted a chance of playing in college, an extra year of development would be crucial. I was young for my grade anyway, so we decided to change schools so I could repeat the eighth grade.

Instead of staying in Atco, we moved to Medford, the town where Shawnee was located. Shawnee didn't accept any students out of town, so the only shot at getting to play at a school like this was to move to Medford. It was also closer to Philadelphia so the work commute was easier for my parents.

I wanted to stay in Atco but also wanted to do what was best for my basketball career. It was the first time I moved though, so the transition was tough. In Atco I wasn't the most popular kid and didn't have many friends. Moving to a new town, I assumed I'd be even lonelier and more of a loser than in Atco.

Fortunately, a few kids from the new neighborhood in Medford eased this transition. Their names were Gil and Kyle, and they called me a few times before I moved into the new house. They were friendly and got to know me, and I appreciated this more than they knew. Once I moved we all became great friends.

When we finally moved to the new house, I got even more focused with basketball. I knew the coming years were extremely important for my future so I wanted to make the most of it. At this time, I made a pact to myself that I would receive a Division 1 scholarship.

My mindset was that if I was going to take basketball seriously, I might as well set my sights high. Not many athletes receive a Division 1 scholarship, but I thought I could do it. Another goal I set was to make the NBA, but a Division 1 scholarship was non-negotiable. Another mini-goal was to attend the ABCD All-American Camp at some point in my career. At the new house there was a hoop in the middle of the driveway and the basement contained a concrete surface that was great for ball-handling drills, so if I didn't achieve these goals there would be no excuses. I had the hoop and I had the space, now I just needed to put the work in.

As I wrote earlier, I believe in subtle signs we can notice if we are aware. Within the first few days of living in the new house I received another. As I was walking up the stairs, the thought occurred to me that I would be taking the same steps four years later as one of the best players on the Shawnee basketball team. The vision was quick and fleeting, but it was also so real and definitive.

In Medford that summer heading into eighth grade, my initiation to hard work commenced. I had worked hard before, but I knew I needed to take it to another level if I wanted to achieve anything of value. Finding a few basketball courts nearby, I sacrificed my summer for sweat.

My shooting drills consisted of twenty makes from seven spots around the three-point line. After that, I'd make twenty from seven spots inside the three-point line. Sometimes I pushed that number to forty or fifty, doing certain basketball moves before the shots. I mixed in ball handling drills, finishing with full court defensive slides. If I didn't work out that day, I'd go to the basement before sleep, turn on the hip-hop station Power 99, and do stationary two-ball workouts for thirty minutes.

Now that I was in Medford, I was also much closer to a recreation center called the Blue Barn. I went there a few times with Kevin growing up, but now it was right down the street. Containing three full basketball courts and a constant stream of players, it was the perfect place to play for hours on end or do my own workouts if nobody was there.

The Blue Barn became my home away from home. On Saturdays, my dad drove me over in the morning and I stayed until late afternoon. It was interesting to see wave after wave of players come in. They'd all come in together, play a few games, then go home. In between waves, I'd shoot free throws, waiting for the next set of players.

I knew that I was playing well that day by how many people asked me, "What grade are you in?" Or, "What school do you go to?" I took pride in getting that question from random people who I'd play against. This meant they were impressed by my skills and wanted to learn more about me. When nobody asked, I knew I was off that day and had to work even harder. My dad finally came back hours later, giving me the thumb in the motion of, "Let's get out of here." When he came, sometimes I was relieved since I was so tired. I'd make my final shot of the day then follow him to the car.

Sometimes I'd see a dad and his son shooting baskets on the other end of the court, having fun and just messing around. I'd think, *Why do I put myself through this? Why don't I just treat basketball as fun instead of work so hard at it?* But then when I completed my workout two hours later, I felt the satisfaction of having worked my butt off, not taking it easy like everyone else had. It's easy to mess around. It's hard to stay disciplined, and I promised myself I'd get that Division 1 scholarship at any cost.

Another way I stayed focused was by often assessing what workout I could do no matter where I was. If we went on a family vacation and stayed at a twenty story hotel, I wasn't excited that we would have room service or a big screen TV. Instead, I'd think, *Yes, they have twenty stories, so I can run the stairs tonight!*

That night, while everybody else was watching a movie, I'd run that staircase until I couldn't run anymore. One year we went to Florida to see my mom's old school. During the middle of the day, my family all went out to a movie while they left me at a gym, getting up shots. They came back from the theater two hours later as I was just finishing up my workout.

That was how I operated.

--

Going into eighth grade, again, I attended Moorestown Friends School, a Quaker school nearby. This school let me repeat the year and provided me with another option if I didn't want to attend Shawnee. However, on my first day, it was a culture shock once again. If I thought going into a primarily African-American school in Winslow was a change, this was the complete opposite.

The first thing I noticed were all the bags laying along the hallway. I asked a person next to me, "What are all these bags doing here?"

He said, "Oh you can just leave your bag here, nobody will take it."

I thought, *What??!! You can leave your bag in the hallway, walk away for an hour and it won't get stolen?? Where am I??*

Since this school was extremely expensive, even for a year, my eighth grade class had only fifty students in it. Our basketball team wasn't that great, but this was my time to shine. Everybody knew everybody since the school was so small, and I got the reputation for being a star athlete before I even played a game.

One major difference about Moorestown Friends was its intense focus on academics. I actually kind of liked this, since it forced me to learn some new things about Shakespeare, Greek mythology, and different styles of writing and learning. It was a Quaker school, so we all gathered in an auditorium every Wednesday to sit in silence for an hour. At any point, someone could speak up and say what was on their mind. Most of us just sat there and played subtle games, like how far we could remove the cushion from the bench without having the whole auditorium hear us laugh. It was immature, but I was only thirteen years old.

I'd get home from school around 7 PM every night, do my homework, watch Seinfeld, then ask my dad to drive me to the Blue Barn. I would have liked to get in more than two hours of practice every night, but I made sure to make the two hours worthwhile. Sometimes I had practice with the team after school, but I'd still go to the Barn from 8-10 PM every night.

For those two hours, I'd play in games or get shots up by myself. My goal was to shoot at least 100-200 shots per day, or at least another few hours playing against higher competition. Because the team at Moorestown Friends wasn't providing me much of a challenge, I loved when I could battle against older, stronger guys at the gym.

I was easily the best player on the Moorestown Friends team, and quickly got a reputation for being one of the best eighth graders in South Jersey. At the end of the season, the Varsity basketball coach sat me down and pitched me why I should come to Moorestown Friends for high school. He knew I had potential but he also knew I was thinking of going to Shawnee.

We talked for about thirty minutes and I responded to his questions as best I could. Zoning out towards the end, I was just going through the motions and trying to be polite. Halfway through I decided that I didn't come to Medford to play at a school where people play sports for fun. My goal was to play Division 1 basketball, and this small Quaker school was not where players received Division 1 scholarships. My best chance for that was at Shawnee.

--

School ended in June and that summer I played on a travel team with a group of skinny white kids from the South Jersey area. Our coach was Joel Ettinger, who had been coaching nearly his entire life. His style was for us to play together, be great teammates, and not worry about how many points we scored. However, when we traveled to New York City to play against teams like the Gauchos, all these things went out the window when they full-court pressed us the entire game. Playing against guys from the inner city who were extremely physical and athletic, we tried to stay focused on playing our game and sharing the ball, but it was mighty difficult. I credit Coach Ettinger for helping us stay focused and not getting overwhelmed when we played teams like these. He also helped me see what a great coach actually was, being a big influence on helping me develop on and off the court.

In my free time, I performed copious amounts of ball-handling drills, sprints, and shooting workouts. I bought an agility ladder, a rope ladder you lay across the ground and run over to develop quickness, which I used as much as I could. At times, my mom saw me doing the agility ladder and came out to try it during the middle of my workout. This made me angry because I felt like workout time was serious, intense, and focused, not time for smiles and happiness. If somebody wanted that, they could get the hell away from me and go watch TV.

I was so intense because I knew Shawnee was going to be a whole new world. The team made it to the South Jersey Championship the year before, and most of their starters were returning to the team. Getting minutes on Varsity was going to be difficult, but I felt that it was possible. I just had to put the work in.

2
MAKING A NAME FOR MYSELF

For most students, the typical path to Shawnee High School was through Medford Middle School. They'd attend Medford Middle in eighth grade, then go on to Shawnee with their group of friends. Moving to Medford from Atco didn't help my social situation at all. Even though Shawnee consisted of over 2,000 students, with about 500 in each grade, I still didn't know anybody except for Gil and Kyle from the neighborhood.

I thought Gil was so cool because he was a little older. He was about 5'8" tall and skinny. He had a bunch of friends who he always went to parties with, but never really played basketball. I attended one or two of the parties with him but never really got into the scene. Regardless, he was a great friend.

I knew guys who played basketball for the Shawnee team, but I wasn't good friends with them. Like the kid from The Sandlot who played with the contraptions in his house all day long, I could play basketball all day without seeing or talking to anyone else. Going into the school year, I thought that wouldn't matter. I knew I was a great player so I thought my basketball skills would make up for it. I thought, *I'm going to come in, be the best player at practice, start Varsity, then become one of the most popular kids at school! Everybody will be surprised and love me because I'm the new kid who is so great at basketball!*

When school started though, it was nothing like what I'd thought. The worst part of the day was lunch time. The rest of the day was easy since I had structure. However, when lunch came, I had nobody to sit with.

I knew one kid I played basketball with during the summer but he had his group of friends and the table was always full. Sometimes I had to kneel down on the hard tiles next to the table and eat my lunch. Also, because I was the new kid, other kids tried to pick on me. I'd just sit there though, trying to act like I couldn't hear them. At one point one of the guys I was sitting with said, "Tyson, just stand up. Once they see you're 6'3" they'll stop picking on you."

Since I was shy and didn't want a problem, I just replied, "No, it's okay."

In those first few months, I rarely said anything to anybody since I didn't want to be seen as uncool. It was hard enough making friends and I didn't want to say or do anything that would give me a bad reputation. I went to school, did my work, and went home.

As the school year progressed I was really excited for practices to start. Here I was at the legendary Shawnee High School with a chance to play on the team. The Shawnee basketball team had a history that went back decades. Dale Adams started coaching at Shawnee in the 80's when they weren't that good. However, over time, he transformed it into a great program, at one point being the best team in the country.

When Kevin and I went to the games growing up, we idolized guys like Brian Earl, Danny Earl, and Malik Allen, who all eventually played professionally. At the end of the games, a few hundred students chanted "WARM UP THE BUSSES!" We imagined how amazing it would be to be on a team like that. After all my imagining, here I was, a freshman at Shawnee, finally getting a chance to try out for the team.

--

A day after Thanksgiving was the first day of tryouts.

The ninth graders tried out for the freshman team, then the Varsity tryouts were afterwards. For a lot of players, this is when they quit for good. When growing up sports is a fun thing to do with friends, but freshman year of high school is when it gets serious. You either are dedicated or not. You're either talented and have potential or you don't. There's no grey area here. You can tell a person's dedication just by the way they run down the court.

Dave and Ken were two guys in my grade. I played basketball with them during the summers and we all took it seriously. They also attended Medford Middle School and played football, so the older players knew of them and they were pretty popular. From an outside perspective, they were slated to be the next faces of the program in the coming years.

On the first day of tryouts, Ken, Dave, and I all tried out for the freshman team together. We were the best players on the freshman team by far, but we already knew that. Once freshman tryouts finished, we had the option to try out for the Varsity team.

Since the only reason I was at Shawnee was to play on the Varsity team, after freshman tryouts I followed Ken and Dave to the larger gym to try out for Varsity. When we walked in, I was star-struck. Along the bleachers warming up were Jason Davis, Wally Brown, Eric Miller, and all the starters on the team. I idolized these guys and got excited that I'd finally be getting my chance to play with them.

We all warmed up until Coach Adams told everybody to begin the team warmup. Following Ken and Dave, we started at the corner of the baseline, doing high-knees to the other end of the court. Since I was an unknown, I was the final one in line.

I started doing a few high-knees, extremely excited to be trying out for Varsity. Suddenly, I felt a tap on my shoulder. I turned my head and saw Coach Adams. He motioned for me to stop.

"Hey Tyson, what are you doing?"

Excited that he knew my name, I said, "I'm trying out for Varsity, Coach."

He replied, "Oh no, we only let the older guys do that."

Puzzled, I stared at him and said, "But Ken and Dave are trying out."

"Tyson, you're only on the freshman team now so you can't try out. Plus, there will be too many players for practice."

I just stared at him, unable to say anything.

He said, "You have to go now."

Not wanting to upset this legendary coach, especially on my first day of practice, there was only one thing I could say, "Okay."

The Varsity team watched me walk back to the locker room with my head down while Ken and Dave continued to try out with the team.

In the locker room, I was angry but there was nothing I could do. I immediately called my dad since he was my ride back to the house.

When he picked up I said, "Hey, can you come pick me up?"

Puzzled, he asked, "What happened? I thought you were trying out for the Varsity team, too."

"I tried, but Coach Adams didn't let me."

Puzzled even further, he just said, "Ok, I'll come get you."

When my dad finally pulled up to the gym, I got in the car and was so angry I was basically screaming.

I said, "How are you not going to even let me try out for the team??!! If I don't make the team that's one thing, but how are you not even going to let me try out??! This is such bullshit!! I should at least be able to try out!! Dave and Ken are in there right now, and they're not that much better than me! This is bullshit!"

My dad was silent as he just drove back to the house. He was probably wondering what the heck was going on too, but didn't say anything and just let me purge my emotion. Once back at the house, I shot in the driveway for an hour just to calm down.

It was my first day of high school practice, but it was also my first hard lesson into the political world of sports.

--

To me, all my hopes and dreams were flying out the window after getting kicked out of Varsity tryouts. Being relegated to only the freshman team hurt, but it hurt even more knowing that Ken and Dave were trying out with Varsity on a daily basis.

How high school basketball works is that if you are a starter on the freshman team, you will most likely play some Junior Varsity, known as JV.

Once you become a starter on JV, then you will most likely get a few minutes per game on the Varsity team. Once you prove yourself in those few minutes, that's when you can start to see real minutes on Varsity, enabling you to possibly score a few points per game. Since I was at the bottom of the pack, I had to work my way up.

I knew guys at other schools who were seeing Varsity minutes immediately as freshman. In my mind, they weren't that much better than me but were already playing Varsity. This made me mad, and even more so that Ken and Dave were already playing with Varsity.

Something I overheard during this time is that other parents thought I'd just get lost in the system. This means that since there are so many kids who want to play on the Shawnee team, playing time gets competitive and it's easy for a player to just get lost in the mix. Eventually, if a player doesn't want to deal with their lack of playing time anymore, they'll just quit or change schools. Lots of people thought this would happen to me since I wasn't raised in Medford and didn't grow up near Shawnee. When I heard that, it fueled my fire even more to prove everybody wrong.

--

Off the court, as the season continued school got easier. Even though I still didn't have many friends, I was known as "the basketball player," which impressed people and helped my shyness. On game days I wore the team colors and got to know a few cheerleaders.

It seemed to me that freshman teams exist for the players who don't take basketball too seriously, but still want to play with their friends. They know they'll never get a scholarship but still enjoy playing. Even though I didn't like this mindset, these guys helped me make some friends. I made sure to do my best and prove I was a better player, yet it still felt good to get along with them.

As the season progressed I eventually got to practice with the JV team. This was great because I still practiced with the freshmen, then with the JV squad. Two practices were better than one, and the JV practices were a lot more intense. The JV coach was a football coach as well, and we did sprints until we were completely exhausted and got cramps in our legs. I compared this to the freshman team who just played for fun, and I felt much more at home with the higher level.

Even though at first I didn't get many minutes during JV games, I got accustomed to how everything worked, and all the subtleties that went into practices and games. However, I still felt like I deserved to play Varsity. Because of this, I pushed myself to work harder than I ever had in my entire life.

After three hour practices with freshman, then JV, I'd go home and shoot outside in the freezing cold for two more hours. After games, I did ball handling drills in the basement for another hour. It made me so mad that I wasn't getting a fair shot at Varsity that I channeled this anger. I didn't complain, I didn't make excuses, and I didn't blame anybody else. I just transformed this emotion into hundreds of shots every day, along with hours of ball-handling and defensive drills. While most guys on the team complained about being tired after two practices in a row, I knew I was heading straight for the hoop when I got home to shoot another 200 shots.

There was a moment, though, that made me question it all. I was outside by myself in the freezing cold, another night getting up a few hundred shots after a double practice. I thought to myself, *Tyson, Why are you doing this? What if this won't be worth it? What if all this hard work won't pay off and you're out here for hours every single night for no reason?*

I didn't have an answer for this, but what came next was a theme that would be recurring throughout my life: Trust. I had no idea if I'd play the next year at all, or if any of this hard work would pay off. But somewhere, deep down, I trusted that it would.

And the real answer? I didn't care. I didn't care what happened that next year because right then, I had a fucking hunger to do anything I could to play on that team. I would have absolutely no regret, putting myself through sacrifice after sacrifice. There was no way I'd get lost in the system, and I'd prove that I was more than just a mediocre JV player. I'd prove it to myself, my family, and everybody watching me that moving to Shawnee was a smart move. I set a goal to achieve a Division 1 scholarship and I was going to achieve it at all costs. Most of all, I made sure I was going to become one of the best players in the state by the time my high school career was finished.

As the games wore on though, it seemed like nothing was changing. One game against Camden Catholic, a rival from the nearby town, I played in the freshman game but not JV. Afterwards, I went up into the crowd with all the other students to cheer on the Varsity team. While everybody around me was excited for the game, I was pissed off, staring at Ken and Dave sitting on the bench while the Varsity team played. Ken and Dave weren't playing, but they had a jersey on while I was up in the stands. During one cheer, a teammate on my freshman team asked me why I didn't have my hands up. I looked at him with disgust, putting my hands up just like all the other students. I felt so disappointed in myself at that moment, being another face in the student section while I knew I should be down on the court.

I was training like a madman at night, but I also made sure to stay on top of my schoolwork. To me, the school part was easy, always having above a B average. I wasn't the smartest person in class, but I knew it was important to do well, especially if I wanted to play on the team. Making friends got easier when I got good grades too, since I could talk to them about schoolwork.

Towards the culmination of the season, I was playing a lot of JV but still hadn't suited up for Varsity. Ken and Dave were getting Varsity minutes and it hurt, but I knew the next year would be different. In the final game of the year, our team traveled to Rutgers University for the State Championship game. I asked the assistant coach if I could ride on the bus to the game with the team, and he agreed. I was relieved since I definitely didn't want to be cheering in the student section during the big game. The team lost, but I sat right behind the bench the entire time. Staring up at the student section, I was so glad I wasn't up there again.

--

As the school year came to a close, I knew I had my work cut out for me. Sophomore year is a big year, since there are new freshmen coming in trying to take your spot, athletes get lost in the system, and things start to get serious. Many of my freshman teammates would quit at this point, unable to handle the pressure and stress of high school basketball.

Sophomore year is when recruiting gets serious, too. If a player just appears on a college's radar senior year, they'll question that player's ability and skill set. But if a college has been watching that player for years, they'll get to know their game and their lifestyle. Having "upside" or "potential" is a great label, especially if you've been consistently improving for the past few years.

Nike recently started a "Summer is Serious" ad campaign. The reason is because during the summer, there are major tournaments all across the country. It's a feeding frenzy for recruiting and rankings, with typical recruiting websites getting over a million views per month over this time period. Also, this is when many athletes receive scholarships from schools.

When the school year finally ended, I took a break for a few days but then started my summer workouts. Nearly every day, I'd put my ball in my bag, run the 1.5 miles to the courts, and do my workout. A main staple of these workouts was full court defensive slides. They consisted of zig-zagging from one end of the court to the other, acting like I was playing defense on a player. I loved doing them because nobody else did them. In my entire life, I never saw anybody willingly do full court defensive slides without a trainer or coach screaming at them to do it. I learned at an early age that if you do what everybody else does, you're going to get what everybody else gets. I always prided myself in doing the thing that other people wouldn't do.

For AAU, the travel team many serious players are a part of between their school seasons, I played with Rick Barrett's Gym Rats, traveling all over the country to places like Los Angeles and Las Vegas. Even there I didn't get much playing time, though, since we had a few older guys on the team. Regardless, it was a great experience to get out of Medford and see what the competition was like across the country.

One thing Rick always said was to treat training as homework and games as the test. All summer, I made sure to do my homework so I'd be prepared for the tests. Sophomore year at Shawnee was my final chance to make an impression, and I had to be prepared.

--

After copious amounts of training over the summer, the stakes were high going into the season. This year was make or break... I could feel it in my bones. If I didn't prove myself, I'd become just another mediocre basketball player who got lost in the Shawnee system.

Once school started, I was more comfortable with the environment and the people. During freshman year I made some friends and didn't feel like the odd person out anymore. A major struggle was who to eat with at lunchtime, but I had some acquaintances from the year before who welcomed me to sit with them. I was relieved I finally had my own place at lunch.

Because of basketball, I became friends with a lot of people I wouldn't have known if I hadn't played a sport. Playing sports isn't quite a fraternity, but it does provide a subtle respect in the eyes of other athletes. If I know a soccer player, there is an immediate conversation piece. Because of this, athletes would know of each other without having actually met.

Since I was more comfortable at this school, I opened up and became a bit of a class clown. I'd do funny things and make jokes, mainly because I didn't want a repeat of the previous year. I pushed the limits of what was acceptable during class but I never went over the line. For example, in one of my classes, while the teacher was writing on the chalkboard I had a competition with another student to see who could stand up and dance the longest without getting caught. It was like the game of chicken, only with dancing.

On the first day of practice, I was immediately playing with the Varsity guys since I wasn't a freshman anymore. This was a great relief because it meant I wouldn't get kicked out of practice. A few seniors from the previous year had left, which opened up a few spots. Everybody was expecting certain other players from the JV team to fill those spots, but I knew this was my opportunity. My only shot was to wiggle my way into the system so I could become one of the trusted players on Varsity.

An interesting thing about the first day of practice is that you can tell who worked out during the summer. From day one, you can sense who put the extra work in versus who took it easy. It's not only how strong they are, how well they play, or how high they jump, it's their subtle confidence level.

21

Will they get mad at themselves for a missed shot, or will they brush it off, knowing they'll make the next one? The players who busted their ass all summer have a higher sense of the game, trusting in the bigger picture and not only worried about what happens play by play.

You can also notice a player's dedication. Will they fight for every rebound or will they just do what is necessary? Will they sprint through the line or will they slow up a few feet from the finish? Will they dive for the ball or just let it go out of bounds? Do they have the fire in their eyes to absolutely destroy you on the court, or are they just there so they can impress their girlfriend during the games? From a summer of heat, self-punishment, and sacrifice, I knew where I stood.

I felt the sting of seeing Ken and Dave play above me during practices, but I took pride in the fact that they weren't getting in the extra work like I was. After practices, I'd be all by myself on the court getting up extra jump shots as they watched me from the side. They'd say to me, "Tyson, you've got too much energy," or "We just practiced for three hours, you don't need to shoot anymore." As they said this, I knew each phrase was just another nail in their coffins.

When games commenced I became a starter on JV. Game after game, I'd average about 10-15 points, while playing solid defense. I knew the work was paying off and I felt it. One day, the JV coach approached me after a game.

He said, "Tyson, you're dressing Varsity today."

He said it very matter-of-fact and handed me my Varsity jersey.

I simply replied, "Thanks" but inside I was screaming with joy. I immediately called my parents, telling them I'd be suiting up for the Varsity game.

--

On the Varsity team, there is a pre-game ritual the players go through that has been around since the early 90's. When Kevin and I went to the packed games years earlier, it was the same ritual. The cheerleaders lined up in a row coming out from the locker room as the song *Crazy Train* by Ozzy

Osbourne blared. When the opening line "Allll abbooaarrddd, Hahahaha," played, the captain of the basketball team ran past the cheerleaders as the crowd would start to cheer.

The players would run around the court once then start doing layups. Once they finished the warmups and got introduced by the announcer, they all dove onto the ground in a circle. I thought this was the coolest part. Kevin and I always talked about how awesome it would be to join them. After a ridiculous amount of hard work and sacrifice, I was finally getting my chance.

In the locker room before my first Varsity game, I put on my warmups as the older guys took notice.

"Tyson's suiting up for Varsity, huh? Nice!"

"Tyson, congrats man!"

I felt so proud of myself. I knew I wasn't going to get any playing time, but the feeling of just suiting up with the team was amazing. We all waited next to the locker room for Ozzy to start screaming. When the guys ran out I was the last one out of the tunnel. Being in the back and seeing all the people cheering us was one of the best feelings in the world. After all my work, I finally make it to Varsity.

We did the lap then went through the layup routine. After they introduced the starters, we all dove onto the floor. Wally, one of the captains, jumped onto my back and started pumping us up.

"Let's get this win today guys! Come on! Let's do it!"

At the end he said, "1, 2, 3….", and we all shouted, "Shawnee!"

We all got up and walked to the bench to wait for the national anthem. Once that was over, we sat down and the game started. Here I was, on the bench for my first Varsity game, as I realized all my sweat and work was starting to pay off.

--

After my first taste of Varsity, there was no turning back. Now that I was so close I needed more. During practice, I focused more intently to make myself look as good as possible in the eyes of the coaches.

The way most players get their shot in sports is if a teammate goes down with an injury. It's an unfortunate way things happen, but just the way it is. If a star athlete gets injured, their backup has to fill their spot for a few games. If the backup performs well, once the star comes back the coaches may keep using the backup instead of the starting player.

A starting forward hurt his foot one game, so he needed to sit out for a few weeks. Since I played his position and was doing well on JV, Coach Adams decided to give me a shot with a few extra minutes during a Varsity game to see how I handled myself.

Since I'd been preparing for this moment for years, when I got into the game I was ready and did well. In the game after, I did even better and got more minutes. The game after that, I played even more. Game after game this continued until I was receiving a solid ten minutes per game on Varsity.

A moment which epitomized my progress was when I was shooting a free throw during one of the home games. Before free throws, the cheerleaders did a cheer then said the person's name at the end. Since nobody knew who I was at the time, they did the cheer, hesitated, then shouted, "Shawnee!"

On the second free throw, I saw them looking around at each other, trying to figure out what my name was. A cheerleader from one of my classes knew me, and she told the other girls my name. Before I shot the second free throw, they did the cheer and said, "Tyson!" I was truly making a name for myself.

When the starting player returned from his injury, he still had his spot on the team, but not at the expense of my playing time. I was a solid contributor now, being trusted to perform my role. I was technically the sixth man, which is the player that gets subbed in right after the starters.

As the season wore on, Coach Adams trusted me more and more. Since I was playing so much during the Varsity games, they didn't want me to play JV anymore. Some juniors and seniors may have resented me for playing ahead of them, but I was quiet and humble so they didn't make a big deal about it. In my mind, I was just struggling to stay on the team.

In school, I was still the class clown and people started to know me from the basketball games. Since I was playing Varsity, I'd sometimes get mentioned during the morning announcements about how many points I had the night before. This impressed people and I'd get even more recognition.

Halfway through the year, I split off from my lunch table to go to another table. The new table was thought of as the "cooler" table, but in reality I was just spending lunch with people I felt I had more of a bond with. The old table might have thought I was getting a big head, but I didn't see it that way. I was just growing and making more friends.

Something else a few people commented on during this time was the difference between school and basketball for me. During the day, I'd make jokes, be a goof, and just try to fit in. Once basketball practice or games hit though, everything changed. I'd be completely serious, not laughing or joking around with anybody. A girl once told me, "Tyson, I can't take you seriously during the games since you're completely different during the day."

Other teammates would say before games, "Tyson, why are you so quiet?"

One thing I learned at an early age from my mom was visualization and meditation. She was really into it, and I started to pick up on what she was doing. Before games, I'd sit in my room and just breathe, calming my thoughts and fears. I believe this definitely contributed to my performance and helped me stay focused.

--

Towards the end of the year, our team was doing pretty well. We had a big game coming up against Winslow High School, which took students from my previous school from seventh and eighth grade. Edgewood had changed its name to Winslow and a few of the guys on the team were my ex-teammates from middle school. We needed to win to get a better seed in the playoffs, and I wanted to play well to prove to my ex-teammates how much better I'd gotten. Winslow also had a pair of twins who were two of the best players in South Jersey, both averaging about 20 points per game.

During warmups, the gym was already packed with cheering fans. When I came off the bench in the first half, I was nervous, but this was my old school so I had to perform. I made a few shots and played good defense as the game stayed close. In the beginning of the second half, I got hit in the eye and lost a contact lens. I didn't have a spare in my bag, so for the rest of the game I played with only one contact lens in. My vision was blurry, but I could still see.

Nearing the end of the game, the score was close. On one particular play, I dribbled down the court and realized nobody was around me. Wide open, I shot a three pointer, hoping I wouldn't air ball it since I only had one contact lens in. I watched the ball hang in the air for a few seconds, then smiled as it swished through the net. I heard the fans in the stands scream with joy as I ran back to the opposite end of the court.

With only a minute left in the game, we were down by one point. An opposing player fouled me, which sent me to the free throw line. I needed to make two shots to put us ahead and only one shot to tie.

Every day I shot free throws between my workouts, so they were second nature to me. I did the same routine every time and swished it nearly every time. Lining up for the first free throw, I did my routine, shot, and made it. On the second free throw, I did the same thing, shot, and made it again. We were up one. On the final play one of the twins got the ball and took the shot, but missed.

We won the game by one point.

Elated that we won, I was told I scored 23 points and made 10 out of 10 free throws. If I missed one free throw, we would have gone into overtime. If I missed two, we would have lost the game. A newspaper reporter interviewed me and Wally, the star point guard and captain, after the game.

The reporter asked me, "Tyson, how did you make so many shots?"

I simply replied, "Well, I just did the best I could."

On the bus back to Medford, I knew this game was the turning point. I had worked all year long for this, and now I scored 23 points and helped the team win an important game. From this point on, I felt I had arrived.

All the while, Ken and Dave were watching from the bench.

--

We made it to the playoffs and won our way to the South Jersey Championship in Atlantic City. The gym was huge, with bleachers stretching about five stories up on both sides. The place was packed with students and fans filling up their respective sides.

Listening to the national anthem before the game, I reflected on how far I had come. A year ago, I was sitting behind the bench of the Varsity team, not even dressing for warmups. Now I was the sixth man, trusted to win games.

When I got into the game I played well, but in the end, we lost by a few points. During the handshakes after the game, I was crying as a photographer tried to snap a few photos of my tears. It was my first time in a situation like this and it was emotional. I dried my tears in the locker room, wondering why nobody else was crying. I thought, *Do they not even care?* Once they started talking about things other than the game, I knew they didn't care as much as I did.

The long trip back to Medford was quiet for a while until everybody started to get over the loss. Losses happen, even if they're in the South Jersey Championship. I felt bad for the seniors since their high school careers were now over, but they had to end at some point. A few of them would be attending college, but only Wally was going to be playing basketball at a small Division 3 school in Philadelphia. The others would just have stories and highlights of their high school basketball careers.

As we got back to Medford, I analyzed the past year and smiled. One year ago I wasn't even dressing on the Varsity team, worried I was going to get lost in the system. However, things have a funny way of working out. The starter got injured, which helped me get some playing time. When I got into the game I performed, which got me more playing time. I helped our team win a few games which proved my talent, and helped me get some playoff experience.

People talk about how there are no shortcuts in life. They say it because it's a cute saying, but I don't think they understand the power of it. There really are no shortcuts in life.

Thinking back to that moment in the freezing cold out in the driveway after a double practice, I thought, *Tyson, what the hell are you doing this for? Will this ever pay off?*

Did the extra work pay off? Yes…but not immediately. The day after my workout I didn't play Varsity. But day after day, week after week, all the extra training built up, until, 365 days later, I scored 23 points and helped the Varsity team win an important game against my old school.

I was proud of myself for what I accomplished, but there was still more to do. I had two years left… and I still didn't have that Division 1 scholarship.

--

About a month after the final game, there was an end-of-year banquet to recap the basketball season and honor all the seniors who were leaving. Since this was the first year I was officially on Varsity, this was my first experience with the banquet. All the players, families, coaches, and boosters attended.

When Coach Adams mentioned me, he said, "Tyson didn't say 'Boo' last year, but now he's the complete opposite."

Everybody laughed. I just smiled. He continued to talk about the next season and who the returning players were. A few seniors were graduating and because of my performance to finish the season, I was definitely on everybody's mind.

As school finished up, my goal was to bring the momentum from the season into the summer. The summer AAU circuit is when scholarships happen, since it's the most intense time of the year for basketball. I'd play with Rick's Gym Rats again, hoping to get some college coaches excited about me.

Rick Barrett's connections went, and still go, far and wide. Somehow, he got in touch with a brother of the legendary Temple player Pepe Sanchez. His name was Fefo, he was from Argentina, and he came to America seeking a basketball scholarship. Since there was nowhere else for him to stay while he traveled around the country playing in basketball tournaments, Rick asked us if we'd let him stay at our house for the summer. It was a new experience but we trusted Rick, so we agreed.

Fefo didn't speak much English, but we understood each other. On one of the first nights at the house, we shot outside for about two hours. He liked to train and it was basically all I did, so we got along. Since he was about two years older than me, he helped open my eyes to life outside of basketball, instead of only worrying about how many hours I would play that day. One time I came home to find Fefo painting the walls of our basement. I asked him why, and he said it was for letting him stay at our house. Little things like this helped me become a better person.

In the beginning of the summer, AAU season started up again. This is when the best travel teams from every area of the country played in the high-profile tournaments. Our team, the Gym Rats, went to a tournament in Washington D.C. Many college coaches and scouts lined the walls, with NBA player J.R. Smith in attendance. In between games, J.R. made half court shots with ease. I thought my shot was good, but his was on a whole different level.

During the tournament games, Fefo and I played on the same team. He was the point guard who dribbled the ball and I was the shooter who he typically passed to. We both played great together in the tournament. After the games ended, Rick said the head coach at the University of Maine, John Gianinni, said he wanted Fefo on the team. Coach Gianinni offered Fefo a full scholarship to Maine. A few days later, Fefo accepted it. I was happy Fefo got the scholarship, but I also wanted one of my own.

About a month after the D.C. tournament, my dad called me. We started discussing Fefo and the scholarship.

A few minutes in, he said, "Well I was talking to Rick, and he said they're offering you a scholarship, too."

I was silent for a second, not understanding what he just told me.

I said, "What??"

"Evidently, they want you and Fefo up there together. They're offering you both a full scholarship because they think you'd play well together. Rick said you should accept it as soon as possible."

I replied, "Wow. Yea, I'll call Rick and accept it."

Still shocked, I called Rick to see if it was real. When I got him on the phone, he told me that it was true; Coach Gianinni offered me and Fefo full scholarships. They thought we had lots of potential with him being the point guard and me being the shooter.

I thought, *Oh my gosh. Did I just get the full, Division 1 scholarship I've been working for??*

After discussing the details, Rick told me I should verbally accept it as soon as possible. I had no other offers at the time, so having one could help get others if necessary. Maine was a solid school with a solid team and I already knew a player who was up there. I told Rick I'd accept it, but I wasn't allowed to officially sign until after my junior season.

Here I was, just finishing my sophomore year of high school, and I achieved my goal of receiving a full, Division 1 scholarship. It was amazing, and I thanked myself for all the hard work I put in.

For the rest of the summer, I went to several tournaments and played my hardest, but the thought of having a Division 1 scholarship was a huge relief. When I saw the coaches lining the walls during tournaments, I wanted to prove I deserved the scholarship, but didn't have the desperation of not having any plans after high school.

As the summer tournaments finished up, I knew I'd be an integral part of the team at Shawnee. I knew I was one of the best players, but I still didn't know exactly how much time I'd get per game. Sometimes, Coach Adams brought in players from different towns or countries to help the team win. Shawnee was a public high school, so these players had to live in the town to attend the school. He'd help these players find a place to live and they'd sometimes take the spots of dedicated players who had been in Medford their whole life. It was unfortunate, but just a part of the political game. I was just hoping he wasn't going to bring in anybody who might jeopardize my playing time. I knew coaches from other schools who paid the families of the athlete to attend their school.

--

When junior year started I had a solid group of friends. To the rest of the students, I was known as "the basketball player" and became pretty popular. Because of this, and because of the scholarship I had, I developed a cocky attitude. I treated everybody around me like they were beneath me. I acted like I was the star basketball player and everybody else was in my world.

In preseason scrimmages, I was easily one of the best players and knew I'd be starting Varsity. My workout intensity lessened, primarily because I knew I was going to get minutes during the season. I had a scholarship, I was definitely going to play Varsity, and I was popular at school. I thought, *What else is there to work for?*

There's a popular saying that says, "You are the average of the five people you spend your most time around." Whether you believe this to be true or not, it doesn't matter. It's a fact. My attitude was bad and I started to hang out with the wrong people.

Instead of hanging out with people who uplifted, challenged and supported me, I started hanging out with people who drank, smoked and wasted time. Since I was older and one of the only people who had my driver's license, they'd constantly ask me to drive them around to different places. On weekends, we'd go to parties and get drunk so I experienced my first hangovers. When they started smoking I knew it was terrible for me being an athlete, but I did it anyway. I thought I was being cool and just wanted to fit in.

Going into the basketball season, I was one of the top ten players to watch in South Jersey. The newspapers were impressed from my sophomore season and everybody thought I had huge potential. Especially after verbally committing to Maine, the fans, coaches, players, and community all expected a huge year from me.

When Varsity practice started the day after Thanksgiving in 2003, it was a disaster. Official practice time was 9:00 AM on Saturday, but it was mandatory that all athletes show up by 8:45 AM to warmup and stretch. I showed up at 8:50 AM, believing that since I was one of the best players, I didn't need to warm up.

When I got in at 8:50, Coach Adams walked right over to me.

As I was putting on my shoes, he stared me straight in the eyes and said, "Tyson, this is how the year's going to start?! I can't believe you right now! You have to be a leader for these guys and you come in late?! I'm tempted to kick you out of practice right now. This is not a good start to the year, Tyson!"

I nodded and knew I messed up, but I didn't think of myself as a leader. I felt I was just another player who got to practice a little late. During practice it was evident who the starters would be, and I was included. A new addition was a freshman he brought in from a different town, but other than him there were no surprises.

For the rest of the year, Coach Adams kept telling me, "Tyson, be a leader! I need you to be a leader!"

When I heard that, the words went in but I had no idea what it meant. The fact is that I didn't know *how* to be a leader. In a way I was still in my sophomore mindset, a newcomer trying to get as many minutes as possible, leaving the leadership to the other guys. Just one year earlier I was struggling to even play on the JV team, now Coach Adams wanted me to be a leader on Varsity? I was honored, but I didn't know what he wanted me to do.

Throughout the season, I kept hanging out with the people who couldn't care less about sports. They were only motivated by how much they would drink on the weekend, not by how many points went up on a scoreboard. When I told them I'd be in the gym shooting for three hours, they laughed at me. Since I wanted them to like me, I sunk to their level and didn't work out nearly as much, conforming to their terrible habits. I developed a bad attitude with my family, treating them like I was much more important than them. I felt I could do anything I wanted and I'd still be the face of Shawnee Basketball.

Halfway through the season, I sprained my ankle. Sitting out a few games, I stepped back to see that our team wasn't very good, and we needed to start winning more games if we wanted to make the playoffs. We were losing to weaker teams and the outlook wasn't promising. However, we somehow snuck into the playoffs to face a much weaker team in the first round. I told the new freshman before the first playoff game, "Shawnee doesn't lose in the playoffs."

Shawnee had a long, storied tradition of going deep into the playoffs while having a passionate fan section every game. This year looked nothing like that tradition. Not many people came to the games and the student section was barren. After taking a step back, I thought it had a lot to do with how nobody knew many of the players on the team. What it really came down to though, was how we were losing so many games. Nobody wanted to watch their team lose.

In the initial half of our first playoff game, the score was nearly tied. As the second half continued, they stayed with us until it came down to the final five minutes of the game. They took a lead, and we had to foul to try to get the ball back. They made all their free throws though, and we ended up losing by ten points. We lost in the first round of the playoffs to a mediocre team. They were obviously excited to have beaten us in the first round on our home floor, but it was terribly disappointing to us.

Overall, the season was a freaking disaster. I was hanging out with the wrong people, not training that hard, and expected someone else to take the reins of the team. I didn't know what being a leader meant or how my attitude rubbed off onto the other players. After the disappointment that I felt, I vowed to make my senior season of high school much different than what I had just experienced. I knew that I let the team, fans, and the program down.

A silver lining from the season was how well I shot at the free throw line. I always practiced my free throws, with my routine being to mix them in throughout my training. On my first free throw of the season, I missed. However, every foul shot after that, I made. Ending the season, I finished with 55 straight makes, missing only one free throw the entire year.

I broke all New Jersey records for free throw percentage in a season, shooting 98% from the line. At the end-of-year banquet for South Jersey, I was awarded with a trophy. The audience gasped when they heard my shooting percentage. It was a great accomplishment, but for me it wasn't too difficult. I just focused, did the same routine I always did, and took the shot.

--

Even though the season was a disaster, I still had decent stats, averaging about 15 points per game with 8 rebounds. This helped me get on the map of a few colleges in the area, as I received letters from places like Delaware, Lehigh, and Manhattan. Since I had a great relationship with the coach at Maine, I knew a player who was already up there and it seemed like a great school, I was going to keep my commitment. However, it was still nice to have options.

On the official signing day for athletes in 2004, I printed out the College Scholarship Acceptance Letter that Coach Gianinni sent me. With the new freshman teammate next to me at my kitchen table, I signed the agreement to attend the University of Maine on a full scholarship. In the fine print, it mentioned they couldn't release me from the team unless I got a debilitating injury or I decided to quit.

I laughed at this and thought, *Who in their right mind would quit a Division 1 program and forego their scholarship?*

I signed my name on the dotted line and faxed it back to the coach. It was official: I'd be attending the University of Maine in Orono with Fefo the following season as a Black Bear. His first year up there would be my senior year at Shawnee, so I was hoping he could introduce me to people and help me out once I got there. Unlike the pros, there was no press conference; only a simple fax stating my intentions for life after high school. I was now the first player since the Earl brothers in the 90's to receive a full, Division 1 scholarship at Shawnee. Thinking about that blew my mind, since I idolized those guys growing up.

A few weeks after I signed with Maine, Coach Gianinni came to my house to meet with me again. When he came, he sat in our living room and discussed his plans for my future. He explained that he knew I was a great shooter, so he saw me fitting in well as a three-point threat who could play strong defense. We both agreed I wasn't the quickest or tallest player so I might not develop into a star, but I would definitely have a role on the team. He was a great guy and even noticed a few things in the house that made me laugh. I knew I probably wouldn't be starting as a freshman, but I trusted that he had my best interests at heart, and he'd work with me to develop my game into the coming years.

The assistant coach, Mike Burden, also gave me a positive view of Maine. Coach Gianinni recruited me, but Coach Burden was the guy I could ask the hard questions about and know he'd be honest. He constantly checked up on me in high school and came to a few of my games. He was there for me whenever I needed to talk to someone, and for that I'm extremely grateful.

After the disaster of a season I just had, I knew I needed to turn things around. I was going to a few high profile camps and tournaments during the summer, so I needed to step my game up. I wanted to prove to myself and to everybody around me that I deserved the scholarship.

There were two All-American camps that I was looking forward to in the summer. The first one was the Pangos All-American camp in Los Angeles. Rick said that if I played well there, he could most likely get me into the big one: The Adidas Superstar Camp in Atlanta.

The Adidas Superstar Camp was Adidas's version of the Reebok All-American Camp which all the top players from across the country attended. Years ago when Nike and Adidas saw the huge success of the Reebok camp, they had to get in on the action so they both created All-American Camps of their own. There would be hundreds of Division 1 coaches there from top schools like Duke, Florida, Kentucky, and Indiana. If I played well enough in front of them, they might be interested in getting to know more about me. Even though I signed to Maine, I would quickly change my mind if Coach K wanted me to come to Duke.

Before I got the chance to play in front of these coaches though, Rick told me I had to perform at Pangos. Since he was putting his name and reputation on the line, if I played terrible at these camps the directors wouldn't trust him to send his players anymore. He told me the story of Gary Lee, a kid who played poorly at Pangos a year earlier but then played great at Adidas. I didn't want to be Gary, so I hoped I'd play great at both camps.

Getting ready for these camps, I got back to the basics. I vetted who I spent my time with and transitioned back into my freshman year workout mentality. This was my last chance to make a name for myself so I had to get my ass in gear. I started putting in two workouts per day again, with shooting in the morning and ball handling at night. Or I'd do sprints in the morning and agility training at night. I trained with the Gym Rats and developed chemistry with the Shawnee players when I could. They thought I was intense, but I wasn't taking any chances.

--

When the weekend of the Pangos Camp arrived, I felt ready. Rick, me, and two other Gym Rats all flew out to Los Angeles. The sky was beautiful, palm trees lined the road and it was much warmer than in New Jersey. Even though the area was gorgeous, Rick repeated over and over again that it wasn't a vacation, it was a business trip.

As I mentioned before, I believe in signs that can give us a premonition of the future. In Mexico, it was the basketball court below the room. In Medford, it was the vision going up the stairs. When Pangos started, another sign appeared loud and clear.

At the start of the camp, all the campers congregated onto the court to get their gear. The director called out names as the players went up to get their jersey. When it came time for my name, he announced, "Jason Hartnett!"

Realizing he probably just messed up my name, I walked over to him and grabbed my jersey, but mentioned to him that my name was Tyson, not Jason. Instead of listening to me and changing the name, he just said, "Ok, that's great," as he started to call the next name. I didn't want to push it or be a nuisance, so I just walked back to where I was sitting.

This was bad for two reasons. First, if I played well, they would have my name as Jason Hartnett which could confuse any scouts or coaches. Second, the indifference was overwhelming. The guy didn't care one bit about what my name was. To him, I wasn't one of the high profile players they brought in; I was just another no-name.

As the camp started, maybe it was the fear of being this year's Gary Lee, or the indifference the director gave me, but I felt off. I didn't have the swag and confidence I usually had when I got on the court. The players they brought in weren't that much better, but I felt a step slower and missed a bunch of easy shots.

In one game, I held my own against a player who was going to Duke, but I didn't separate myself from him. If I completely outplayed him, that would raise a few eyebrows from the sidelines, but I didn't. I played mediocre. At the hotel after games, the guys wanted to go to the mall but I just wanted to stay in the room. Only when they urged me to come out did I relent. I was in a weird funk and I didn't know how to shake it.

On the final day of the tournament, Rick saw that I didn't play well. In the car going back to the airport he said, "You're my this year's Gary Lee. You played bad here, but now you have to play great at Adidas. I'll get you in there, but you CANNOT fuck it up. Do whatever you have to do, but you better not fuck it up."

Back in Jersey, the only thing on my mind was how I could play great at the Adidas Camp. There was two months left, so I had a solid amount of time to train. Every day, I'd run to the courts, do the shooting drills, then do ball handling drills for hours in the afternoon. I wasn't taking any chances, making sure I'd be completely ready.

There was a lot at stake: My reputation, Rick's reputation, and the overall pride I had for my game. The players would be a lot better than Pangos, so I had to get myself ready.

--

All the weight was now on my shoulders.

In the past, many players have made or broken their careers at a camp like this. Lenny Cooke got demolished by Lebron James back in high school and he never recovered. Tracy McGrady went from a no-name to a first-round NBA Draft pick because of how well he played. Countless others received Division 1 scholarships or at least put their names on the map because of their performance at a camp like this.

A few days before I left, my dad called me and said, "Ryan and Tony aren't going to the Adidas camp, do you still want to go?"

I thought, *Are you kidding me?! I've been training for this moment for years, and you're wondering if I don't want to go to this camp just because my Gym Rat teammates Ryan and Tony aren't going?!*

Instead, I politely responded, "Yes, of course."

I took the plane out of Philadelphia and headed to Suwanee, Georgia. The gym was right outside of Atlanta, and the camp was actually featured in the book <u>Play Their Hearts Out</u> by George Dohrman.

Getting to the Adidas Camp on the first day had me feeling like a king. When I got to the airport, a bunch of basketball players huddled around a guy holding a sign that said, "Adidas Superstar Camp."

I walked up to the guy and, with a touch of pride in my voice, said, "I'm here for the camp."

He responded, "Ok, hang with these guys. We'll be leaving shortly."

When the bus came, it was filled with TVs and fancy seats. I felt like I was in the NBA. At the hotel, I saw Rick sitting in the lobby with a few of the camp directors.

I walked over to him and said, "What's up Rick?"

"What's up Scooby Doo?"

As we locked eyes, there was an unspoken message from him saying, "Don't fuck this up."

We talked for a minute then I went up to my room where I had a queen-sized bed. I thought I had the room to myself, but another player named Manadu came in twenty minutes later. He was a few inches taller than me at 6'8" and brought an older guy with him who looked like his agent. Every night, that guy slept on a chair in the room with us.

In the elevators of the hotel, I noticed the name badges of guys I only read about in magazines and scouting reports. These were guys who committed to high Division 1 schools, like Michael Flowers (Wisconsin), Javaris Crittenton (Georgia Tech), and Tyler Smith (Tennessee). This proved to me that the camp was the real deal, and I had to play at my peak.

It was a unique experience walking around with people taller than me, but it felt good. Typically, I'd be the tallest person wherever I went, especially at high school. For the first time in my life, I felt short.

As the camp started, we were required to wear the gear they provided us. When we did drills in the morning, I wore all the gear but didn't wear the shoes they gave me. I had my own Adidas shoes that I thought would be fine. I was comfortable in these, and didn't want to risk getting any blisters from a new pair of shoes. There was a lot riding on this camp and I didn't want a few new blisters to affect my performance.

During our drills, a camp director approached me and asked why I wasn't wearing the Adidas shoes they provided.

I said, "I didn't know it was mandatory that I wear them."

Looking pissed off, he said, "Ok here, take these."

He gave me a new pair of shoes. I quickly took off mine and put on the new ones. Later in the day, I saw Rick and told him what happened.

He said, "You've got to be shitting me."

Evidently, when he was talking with the other directors, they were discussing a kid who didn't wear his Adidas shoes. Rick said he just kept hoping it wasn't me, because they would have probably sent me home. When he found out it was me, I didn't hear the end of it.

In the beginning of each day, we did drills and exercises. In the afternoon, we played games. At one point, Coach K from Duke watched one of my games in the afternoon. I was nervous, but I played pretty well in front of him. I made a few shots, passed well, and played great defense. Afterwards, I was hoping he'd come up to me and say, "Tyson, I *need* you to come to Duke on a full scholarship. I have the papers all filled out right here." Unfortunately, that didn't happen, but it felt great to be playing in front of such a high profile coach.

As the camp wore down, I didn't embarrass Rick like he feared I might. I averaged 10-15 points per game and he watched a game in which I made two three pointers and a two pointer with no turnovers. These guys weren't that much better than me, they were just stronger and more athletic. Once I compensated for that, I did well, held my own, and played how I knew I could play. All the hard work paid off because I knew I could hang with the best players in the country.

On the last day of the camp, there was an All-Star Game in which many future NBA guys played. Sitting by myself on the sideline watching, I soaked in the moment, realizing I was accomplishing everything I wanted to achieve. I earned my spot at the Adidas All-American Camp, I played great, and I had a Division 1 college scholarship going into my senior year of high school.

After the tournament, all Rick said was, "You're my this year's Gary Lee." He meant that I didn't play well at Pangos but stepped up at Adidas. That was the best I was going to get from him, so I took it as him telling me, "Great job, Tyson."

I was proud of myself that I didn't let him down.

--

After the Adidas Camp I played in a few more AAU tournaments until the end of the summer. Even though I didn't play that great in the tournaments, I still had the satisfaction of having a full, Division 1 scholarship.

During one AAU tournament, I noticed a scout I saw at all my games. An older Irish guy with blond hair, he watched me play badly one game. After that, I never saw him again. He probably reported back to the head coach that I wasn't worth looking at, and they probably told him not to pursue me anymore. It hurt to know that school wasn't interested in me, but I already had a scholarship anyway.

Arriving back at Shawnee, I felt an immense sense of pride in my game. I held my own against the best players in the country that summer, so playing against the weaker competition in Medford was going to be a breeze. I was an All-American, and that's the confidence I felt going into the season.

Before the start of every season, the team had optional preseason workouts on the track after school. We'd do agility workouts, sprints, and even run a few miles. In past years, nobody really took them seriously, but I was in charge of them this year. I was going to make sure I'd finish my high school career on top and these workouts were an integral part. I knew success and wins didn't just happen, they were the reward from months of training.

On the track one day, a moment proved that our team was going to be ready for the season. We all lined up, ready to start our sprints. The football team was practicing on the field right next to us and our whole team took off in a sprint at the same time.

On the field, I heard a football player sarcastically yell out, "Yea! Shawnee basketball! Woo!"

He was trying to make fun of us, but I wasn't having it. After everything I'd been through up to that point, I wasn't going to let a sarcastic comment from a random football player slow us down. I was Tyson, the All-American basketball player who had a Division 1 scholarship, and I was taking this team to the Promised Land whether they liked it or not.

--

On the first day of practice I was more than ready. After battling against the best players in the country all summer, the small town athletes in Medford didn't stand a chance. I was determined to prove that I deserved the scholarship, deserved the All-American title and deserved to be the leading scorer on the team.

The first game of our season was against a major rival and the stands were packed. We won the game, I had 20 points, and we sent a message that we were not a team to be taken lightly. I led the charge and everybody else played their role. As games continued, we stacked up win after win.

Things were great on the outside, but there was ugliness on the inside. I felt like Coach Adams didn't like that I had gotten a Division 1 scholarship, and especially that I got it from playing with Rick. I thought maybe he felt like I wasn't being loyal to him.

When the team chose the captains at the beginning of the season and I was one of them, one of the guards said, "How is Tyson a captain?"

Adams responded, "I have no idea…*you* chose him." I overheard this but didn't say anything.

As the season continued and we kept stacking wins, Coach Adams would say things to me that made me question whether he even wanted me on the team. I constantly heard, "Tyson, stop being so selfish," during practices and games. One time he said the coach at Maine called him to ask how I was doing. Instead of saying it was a great conversation and he supported me, Adams just said, "Well, I'm not going to lie to him. I'm going to tell him the truth about you."

I started second-guessing myself all the time. I thought, *Am I doing something wrong here? Am I being a horrible leader and teammate??* I was confused and nervous just to go to practice sometimes for fear of what he'd say to me.

During Christmas, Fefo came down from Maine for winter break. They only had a few days off but it was great to see him again. We talked about the team, the practices and what it was like up there, since I'd be with him in a few months.

In the middle of our discussion, he surprised me by saying, "I'm not going back. I'm miserable up there. I hate it. I'm going back to Argentina."

I thought, *Are you kidding me? You have a Division 1 scholarship and it's a great school! What's not to like?!*

I asked him why he didn't like it, and he just said it was too cold and he didn't like playing at a Division 1 school. When he left, I wondered why the hell he would quit. This was a huge opportunity. Thousands of kids across the world would kill for a Division 1 scholarship while he was just giving it away. It made no sense to me but I respected his decision. I thought, *Maybe he just doesn't care as much as me.*

On the court, we still hadn't lost a game going into the twentieth game of the season. During this matchup, we played a local Catholic school, one of their star players being a kid I grew up playing with. He was heading to Albany University, a team in the same conference as Maine so we both had a huge amount of respect for each other. We lost by one point for our first loss of the season. He and I each had about 20 points.

We were definitely making the playoffs, but because of Coach Adams, I didn't even care. I just wanted the season to be over with as quick as possible. I didn't even want to look at him, much less be his starting player and win games.

Before one of the final practices in the regular season, one of the other starters didn't want to come to practice. I asked him why, and he told me he didn't want to see Coach Adams anymore. He said it was just too much for him. I went to his house with my teammate and we basically dragged him out, telling him we would win for us.

In the playoffs, we won game after game until we got to play in the South Jersey Championship in Atlantic City. The last time I was there was two years before, playing as a sophomore trying to get as many minutes on Varsity as I could. Now, I was one of the top players in the state with a Division 1 scholarship in hand.

The game was against Atlantic City High School. Since they were the home team, every seat was taken. We still had a huge fan section but their supporters far outweighed ours. After our usual warmup routine and during the national anthem, I reflected on the moment. This was my chance to win a South Jersey Championship, something I hadn't yet accomplished.

Their team was taller and more athletic, but we tried to make up for it with fundamentals. We played a tight zone defense and the score was nearly tied at halftime. They were a quick team so we had to box out and help each other on defense. Through three quarters, we were still even.

When five minutes remained in the game, both sides of the gym were screaming and chanting at each other. It was madness, but I loved it more than anything in the world. These regular people had turned into crazy, bloodthirsty animals, all because of us on the court below.

With two minutes remaining, Atlantic City's athleticism and conditioning took over. They got too many rebounds and their defense was great. The final score showed them having a five point advantage and we lost the game. With that, my high school basketball career was officially finished.

Unlike two years ago on the same court, I didn't have any tears streaming down my face. In fact, I was relieved for the season to be over with. I didn't want to look at or deal with Coach Adams one more day, even if our team *was* doing so well. Atlantic City was a great team to lose to since they had respectful players. When they won, they didn't act cocky, but instead were humble as they congratulated us on a game well played.

We all filed into the locker room as I took off my jersey for the final time.

--

After the loss, I didn't want to do anything for a long while. I was exhausted physically, but more so, mentally.

At the culmination of every season, the newspapers pick their top five players for each position in South Jersey and New Jersey as a whole. Since we had a 25-1 record throughout the regular season, with me being the leading scorer and rebounder on the team, I figured I'd be on all the rankings. This was important to me because it would be icing on the cake for the thousands of hours of work I put in. From getting kicked out of tryouts on my first day of freshman year to leading this team deep into the playoffs as a leading scorer, I felt I deserved any accolades that would come my way.

However, it wasn't meant to be.

When I opened the newspaper to see where the reporters ranked me, I was nowhere to be found. I wasn't in any of the major newspapers at all, when I felt I was easily as good as the other players who made the first teams. After the shock of not making any of the teams, I thought about what may have happened.

Before the newspapers made their final rankings, they typically called the coaches to get their input. I had a feeling that when the newspapers called Coach Adams, he didn't vouch for me. The reporters had no choice but to believe him, so they may have kept me from all the rankings. While I was expecting to go to Maine being an All-State or at least All-South Jersey player, officially it wasn't the case.

I didn't confront Coach Adams about the rankings because I didn't want to deal with him ever again. On the final day I'd ever need to see him, we had to return our warmups and jerseys to the coaches, all washed. I brought the bag of clothes, but I couldn't even go into the same room as him since I didn't want to look him in the eye. Later that day, I got an angry call from him because I didn't place the bag in his hands. It felt like a nightmare I couldn't get out of.

Once I came down from the emotions of the season, I started to tell my parents about what was going on. They had no idea. My mom told me to take a pen and notebook and just write everything down. In the basement of the house one night, I started writing. Thirty-five pages later, I finished. I walked upstairs and asked her if she wanted to read it.

She said, "Only if you want me to."

I pondered it for a minute then replied, "Okay... read it."

I left her the notebook and I went back downstairs to the basement. Five minutes later, she came down crying, telling me she had no idea this was happening. I said it was going on all season, and the other guys were experiencing it, too.

That weekend, I was sitting in the living room, still in a mind-fuck from the season. I could barely think since I had Adams' words in my mind telling me, "Tyson, you're so selfish! What's wrong with you?!"

My mom knew I was in pain. She handed me a piece of paper that had a saying on it describing what it meant to be a warrior. It was only about five paragraphs long, but halfway through it I just started crying my eyes out. My dad walked in and just watched me, wondering what was going on.

In discussing what I should do to process my emotions, we brought up the idea of having a meeting with Coach Adams. A few of the Shawnee staff offered to moderate. I wanted to look Adams in the eye and have a man-to-man conversation about how I felt.

After a short time I began to have second thoughts about a meeting. I thought, *Do I really want to see him again?* While deeply deliberating it, I stopped in to a 7-11 to get a Sprite. As I pulled in, one of the Shawnee staff members was getting into his car.

He said, "Hey Tyson, did you still want to do that meeting with Adams?"

I was put on the spot and had to make an immediate decision. I replied, "Yes, I do."

He said, "Okay, I'll set it up for next week."

Preparing for the meeting, I brought with me the thirty-five pages I wrote down. I specified certain areas which I thought had the most impact. I hoped that would get it out in the open so he could understand where I was coming from.

On the day of the meeting, we walked into the conference room with my mom and dad accompanying me. With about six administrators sitting around us, I positioned myself across from Coach Adams in the middle of the table. In front of him, a notebook was placed on the desk.

I thought, *What the hell is that for?*

A staff member began the meeting by thanking everybody for coming. Then they said, "Okay Tyson, what would you like to talk with Coach Adams about?"

I started with, "I'm wondering why you were such a jerk to me."

From there, I brought up different instances and scenarios about what I wanted to say. However, a minute into the discussion, I knew it was going nowhere. For everything I said he had a rebuttal of his own.

In one scenario, I told him it hurt when he called me an outcast. He responded by saying, "Well, you are an outcast. You rarely hang out with the team."

Another time I asked him why he always called me selfish. He said, "Because you only focus on yourself too much."

I felt like he put everything back on me, about how I was wrong for every scenario. We went back and forth for another fifteen minutes until I realized I was just wasting my time. Annoyed at the whole thing, my mom asked him some questions, with my dad ending by saying, "After everything we've done for you, this is how you treat us? What the hell is wrong with you man?"

At that, the board members said it was time to finish up, since it was obvious that my dad was getting too angry. As we walked out, I still looked at Adams straight in the eye and shook his hand. A few days later, the board members said they had a lot of respect for me when I shook his hand, considering the circumstances.

As the school year wound down, I took some time off from basketball. For four years, I had constantly been going hard, looking forward to the next tournament or camp. Since I was finished with high school I wouldn't be playing any AAU anymore, only getting ready for college in the fall.

Looking back, the vision walking up the stairs when I first entered the house in Medford came true. I became one of the best players at Shawnee and the first to receive a Division 1 scholarship in over a decade. I realized that all the work I put in and all the sacrifices I made paid off.

--

When school ended, physically I was recovered but mentally I still had a ways to go. At the Blue Barn, I'd replay the lyrics from Eminem's song "Renegade" in my mind over and over, "Do you have any clue of what I had to do to get here? I don't think you do…"

Since I needed to rest, my routine was terrible. I'd stay up until about 2 AM every night then sleep in until noon or 2 PM some days. All I wanted was rest and didn't even want to think about training for Maine. Slowly though, I eased myself back into training, but it wasn't to the extent of past summers. Even my parents didn't push me since they knew I was still recovering from the long season.

Towards the end of the summer, there was an orientation at Maine for new athletes and students. Since I was going to be a new student-athlete, and literally had nothing else to do, I figured it would be smart to get a sense of the school. I flew up there with my mom and dad and we stayed at a hotel while I did the daily activities of meeting people and learning about the area.

I didn't really know anybody, but found a few people who were from the Philadelphia area. We immediately bonded and I told them I was going to be playing on the basketball team. When I said that, their eyes lit up. I could tell they thought that was so cool.

Later in the day, I met with the new head coach of the basketball team, Dennis Stewart. I was nervous coming into this situation since the coach who recruited me, John Gianinni, took a new coaching job at La Salle University in Philadelphia the year before. Dennis Stewart had been his assistant coach and got promoted.

When we met with Coach Stewart, he talked a lot about the team and the new players but not much about me. I asked him where I fit into the system and he just said, "We have a lot of great players and you'll have to work for your spot."

Since I was the new freshman coming in and I agreed with his statement, I gave him the benefit of the doubt. Either way, I wanted to trust him, and was more than willing to work for my spot on the team. At the end of our conversation, he told me that I was the first basketball player to ever attend the new student orientation. I thought, *How is that possible? It's an orientation to get a new student acclimated to a new school…why wouldn't someone go?*

Looking back, he seemed to say it in a way that expressed, "I don't know why you came up here."

After the orientation, I trained in Medford for the beginning of my freshman year of college. I was excited, and especially excited to get away from South Jersey. Once August came, I started to work out harder but didn't want to be exhausted for the start of the year since I knew they would put us on an intense training program.

When the weekend of the move-in came, I said bye to my friends and packed up the necessities from my room. I was excited to start a whole new life, in a whole new state, with brand new people.

3
A HARSH REALITY

My mom, dad, and I took a plane up to Bangor, Maine in early September. Since my younger sister had school, she stayed at home for the weekend. At the hotel in Bangor, we woke up at 7 AM on the day of the move-in and got ready to bring my belongings to the dorm where I'd be living. Since I was an athlete, the coaching staff got me in one of the best dorms on campus, and a room with a shower in it that was right next to the gym. It was on the first floor of the building and was a typical dorm style, with brown walls and hard tiles beneath our feet.

As we brought my stuff from the car into the room, my roommate Phil was already there. Looking around at other students moving in, most of them were skinny, pale, and young. Phil, however, was the opposite. Hailing from Cameroon, Africa, he stood at 6'6" tall with muscles like a bodybuilder. At the beginning of high school, I was 6'3" tall, but now I was 6'6", weighing about 210 pounds. We were the same height but he was much stronger. He stood up as I walked into the room and, with a French accent, said, "Hey man, what's up? I'm Phil. It's nice to meet you."

We embraced with a handshake and I felt the strength in his hands. I thought, *Shit, I hope I'm not going to have to battle against him every day.*

I introduced my family and we talked for about ten minutes as I put my stuff on the bed. He didn't have many things and I didn't either, so we didn't overwhelm each other with material items. After a few minutes I realized *why* I didn't have many things, and it was because I forgot two suitcases in Medford. They were both full of clothes so I now had to buy some shorts before practice started.

Once we got my stuff set up, my parents left for the day, telling me they'd come back tomorrow so we could buy a few necessities. Once they left, it was just me and Phil in the room as I experienced my first taste of freshman independence.

He then said to me, "Hey man, we've got practice today, but it's not mandatory."

I thought, *What?? I just got here...they're making us practice already??*

Instead, I replied, "Okay, yea, I don't think I'm going to go. I want to get accustomed to the new place."

We started talking about each other and I jokingly asked him if he rode elephants to school, being from Africa. He laughed and replied, "Yes, but mainly we ride lions."

About thirty minutes later, one of the coaches came to the dorm to say hi. He mentioned the optional practice but then told us the practice tomorrow was mandatory. Phil and I both agreed that we'd be there on time. That night, we met some of the other guys on the team and figured out how to get to the different buildings for class.

The next day, I went with my parents to buy some clothes and other necessities for the room. The only shorts the store had were little Russell basketball shorts which weren't very stylish. I envisioned all the guys coming in wearing cool Jordan shorts, while I was wearing small, tight Russell shorts as they laughed me out of the gym. I didn't want to make a fool of myself on the first day, but I didn't have a choice.

When it was time for my parents to head back to Medford, I embraced both of them, thanking them for helping me out. With my mom crying, they walked out of the room, closed the door, and I was left alone for my first college experience.

I started smiling as Phil said, "Hey, you're happy man, huh?"

"Heck yea man, this is awesome."

I *was* happy, but I was also up there for a reason. I was treating it as a business trip as Rick always said. I wasn't at this school to drink or party, but to grow my basketball career and make a name for myself outside of

Medford, New Jersey.

--

A few hours after my parents left, Phil and I went to our first practice. While all the other students headed straight for the liquor store to get drunk on their first night of college, we had to practice. From these first moments, I knew I wasn't going to live the typical college lifestyle. I had the feeling, but I didn't realize the extent of it until later.

Most of my teammates were at this practice, which was a meet and greet more than anything else. We played in the main gym, which looked like the Hoosiers arena, with huge walls on each side. We got accustomed to the locker-room, and it was really cool seeing the nametag above my locker. They told us that during practices we would be wearing a grey shirt with blue shorts, and to put our dirty laundry on hooks so they could wash it for us. I was relieved when they said this since I only had the small Russell shorts to wear. For shoes, they provided us with two pairs of New Balance basketball shoes and said if they got ruined we could get more.

We received our training schedule for the next few weeks, with separated workout times according to what position we were. Guards trained with each other during certain hours, then big men went through their own workouts. I was more of a shooter so I'd be playing with the guards while Phil trained with the bigger guys.

At this point, everything felt so real. I was finally with a bunch of high-level athletes who were dedicated to improving every day. I loved to work out, so two or three workouts a day was heaven to me. Add in that we got free shoes, clothes, and a cool locker, and I felt right at home.

The next day we had our first individual workout. Training with the guards, we played in the Fieldhouse right next to the gym since the actual gym was being used. For a half hour, we did different drills and I got tired pretty quickly. I was in decent shape but for the month leading up to September, I didn't work out that hard since I knew we would be put through intense workouts with the team. My mindset was that I didn't want to be burnt out by the time I got up there.

Once we finished the drills, we played full court three on three. At this point, I was exhausted, and it showed. This was my first practice with the team and I was sucking wind. The coaches and players could see it, and were probably wondering how I got a scholarship to play up there if I was that bad. I was playing so bad that on one play, I passed the ball directly to the other team.

On defense one play, the player I was guarding stood in front of my teammate so the guy with the ball could get an easier shot. I screamed out, "Screen!"

The assistant coach immediately chimed in, "Tyson, yelling 'Screen' is only half the battle. You have to tell him what you want him to do, whether it's to go under, over, or switch!" *(Editor's note: To this day, every time I play basketball I remember this scenario whenever my guy sets a screen on a defender, and it brings me back to this first practice.)*

On offense, I couldn't get to the hoop easily since the guy guarding me was a lot stronger. The coaches probably noticed this and I felt my chances of getting any playing time during the year slip away moment by moment. Finally, the other team won. The coaches then told us to shoot a few free throws to cool down. I shot mine quickly then ran off into the empty locker room.

All alone in the locker room, I started to cry. I knew at that moment I was screwed. This was the worst possible first impression I could make. I played terrible, felt overmatched and was out of shape. These guys were very good and wouldn't give me an inch on offense or defense. I went to the bathroom and put my head in the sink, crying even louder.

When I looked up I saw Armin, the opposing player during the three on three game, staring at me. He said, "Hey man, you'll be okay. Last year, I cried every day after practice for the first three weeks. It's hard, but you'll be okay. Trust me."

I appreciated his words, but I thought he was just trying to calm me down. He didn't know what I was going through, and it was even more embarrassing that he was seeing me cry on the first day of practice. I was Tyson, the All-American and Division 1 athlete, yet these guys were busting my ass during a simple three on three game. I felt like I didn't deserve to be there. I felt like I was a fluke.

Eventually, I calmed down, just as the other guys walked in. I wiped my eyes, got changed and walked out of the locker room, contemplating just getting a plane ticket and flying back to Medford.

--

As classes started and practices continued, I started to realize how overmatched I really was. I was a skinny, not very athletic 18-year-old kid playing against 25-year-old men with kids and wives. Were they going to let a young freshman kid take their spot on the team? Hell no.

I called Rick to tell him what was going on. Since practice didn't officially start yet, I thought it wasn't too serious that I wasn't doing well. He told me, "Are you serious? They're putting their team together *now*. Whatever you do *now* reflects on what happens the rest of the year."

His words hit me hard, making me realize I was even more screwed than I thought. I wasn't playing well in practice, and no way would I become a completely different player just because the practices were "official." My hopes were diminished but I was still on the team so there was a glimmer of hope. The weekday workouts of individuals and strength training gave me a taste of what official practices would be like, but they still didn't completely prepare me for it.

That, I had to experience for myself.

--

On the first day of practice in my college career, I was scared shitless. If individual workouts were any indication of what was to come, I was about to get beat down and have my ass handed to me.

On a cold, cloudy Saturday morning on October 15, 2005, it started. Practice officially began at 8:00 AM, about the time most college kids were in dream land, sleeping off their hangovers from the previous night. At 7:00 AM, I woke up and walked around campus looking for a place to get some food. None of the dining halls were open and we had nothing to eat in the room.

As I headed to the main part of campus, I got a text from my dad saying, "Good luck today."

I appreciated it, but a simple text message wasn't going to help me play better or relieve my fears. Nearing the food court, I saw Olli, a 6'10" senior on the team.

He said in his deep Finnish-English accent, "You ready for practice today?"

Nervously, I replied, "Yea, as ready as I can be." I found the only open café on campus, ate, then headed over to the gym.

When I walked into the locker room, most of the guys were already gearing up. I felt like we were all going to war, but a war against each other. For many of these guys, basketball was all they had in life. Getting this Division 1 scholarship provided an out from the town they were in, and they'd do anything they could to keep it and make the most of it. Anybody who got in their way was theirs to destroy. Yes, we were a team, but everybody was out to get theirs as well.

In the locker room, I never said much. The loud ones talked about all the girls they were with or anything else that came to their minds. Like in high school, before practices and games I would be very quiet, trying to stay as focused as possible. Wrapping my ankles in the bulky braces they made us wear, I proceeded to put on my grey shirt, blue shorts, and New Balance shoes. I tied my laces tight and took a deep breath. On the outside, I was ready for practice.

In short order, the coaches came in and told us to head to the court. We all filed out to begin our warmup and performed a few exercises to get our bodies moving. After that, we partnered up and sat in a circle at half court, stretching for ten minutes. A senior called out a stretch then one player performed that stretch on their partner. Some guys took the stretching seriously while others didn't. Me? I knew stretching was one of the most important parts of the game so I made sure to take it seriously.

When the ten minutes counted down, official practice began. We started off with regular drills any team would do then transitioned into games. Full court sprints were added in to get our conditioning up. After about four hours of games, drills, sprints and free throws, practice finally ended. I was exhausted, but I survived and didn't quit. Yes, I got beat down, embarrassed, and man-handled, but I stuck with it. Honestly, I didn't know how I was going to practice like this day after day, but I just told myself to take it one practice at a time.

If I was going to survive the season, I needed to improve quickly. The only way I knew how to do that was to work harder than everyone else. Once we got our practice schedule, that's when I started to put the extra work in. If we had individual workouts at 7:30 AM, I got to the gym at 7:00 and shot for thirty minutes. Initially, I was working out at night time after everybody went home. When I told Rick, he said that was the dumbest thing I could do.

He said, "Look man, if nobody sees you work out, it's like it never happened. Make everybody know that you're putting in the extra time."

I loved shooting at night but if I wanted to look good, I'd have to start working out when the coaches could see it. This was called the political game and these were the rules. If an assistant coach saw me doing sprints by myself at 6:30 AM when there was no workout that morning, it would look very good for me. Thinking it would help, that's what I did. When I went to the gym, I made sure there was at least one assistant coach able to see me workout, since their offices overlooked the court. When I did ball handling drills, I made sure to pound the balls extra hard so they all knew I was in the gym.

I adjusted my habits but it was a struggle. Practices were tough and I always had to be on point. If we didn't make a time during a sprint or if we missed a shot in a certain drill, we had to start it all over again. Being in shape was the most important part, and I had come to college not ready for it. I knew practices would be difficult but I didn't think they'd be *this* difficult. From movies and TV, I saw college as a place with wild parties, girls, and an easy lifestyle. Being an athlete, it was the complete opposite.

This was my first time away from home and that didn't make the situation any easier. When I looked at my roommate Phil, it seemed everything was easy for him. He played well in practices and the sting of being away from home didn't seem to hit him as hard.

I brought a Philadelphia Eagles calendar and, week by week, I marked off the days as they passed. This gave me visual confirmation that even though it was hard, I was making progress and getting through it. Once I got out of October, I reached November. After November, it was only a few weeks until I'd be able to go home for Christmas.

Towards the end of October, my dad called and said he and my mom were most likely going to get a divorce. I thought, *What?!*

He explained that she wasn't happy with him anymore, but he thought they were just going through a rough patch. I didn't really think they would actually get divorced, but that started to weigh on my mind, too. When I called my mom, she told me that things were changing and she just didn't want to be with him. I tried to figure out what the problem was, but she seemed set in her ways. I couldn't talk her out of it and things weren't looking good. I also felt like it was partly my fault because I couldn't be there for them.

On the court, I started doing the extra work to show that I cared, like getting to practices early and staying late. I could tell some of the guys were impressed but it didn't help me get any more playing time in scrimmages. Even though I was working harder, it seemed there was nothing to show for it except being more tired during practices.

The interesting thing about basketball is that there aren't any surprises from practice to games. If you're one of the starters in practice, you will most likely start during the game. If you are not even in the top ten in practice, you will most likely never see a minute during the season. At that point, I was at the far end of the bench.

One poignant moment occurred which made my role crystal clear. Most of the team was on the other side of the court being addressed by Coach Stewart. I was standing at the other end next to Jesse Keith, one of the other guys who didn't play, and it seemed Stewart didn't even know we were there. Jesse and I just looked at each other, both of us feeling the instant bond of being the guys at the end of the bench, as we ran over to join our team on the opposite end.

It hurt that I wasn't playing at all but there was nothing I could do. I was overmatched and every day of practice proved this even further. The fact that I was on scholarship made me even more ashamed of not playing at all, since they were paying me to be there.

A few weeks before games started, Coach Stewart pulled me aside before a scrimmage and said he thought redshirting would be the best option for me. Redshirting is when a player doesn't play that year for medical reasons, yet they still keep the year of eligibility. Since every athlete has only four years of college eligibility, this is a loophole teams use to keep players on the team five, sometimes even six years. Redshirting can only be done once, however.

When Coach Stewart told me this, he was basically saying there was no way I'd play that season so I may as well keep my year of eligibility. I wanted to play but I saw his reasoning. I'd rather keep a year of eligibility instead of only playing five minutes the entire season. In my mind though, I felt like a failure.

In high school, when I saw guys who went to college and redshirted, I judged them as not being good enough to play. Now, here I was, redshirting my freshman year. I wanted to prove to the people back at Shawnee that I could play at the Division 1 level, but so far it wasn't happening.

Regardless, I agreed to the redshirt. A positive aspect about this was that I didn't have to worry about playing in games, which gave me the opportunity to work extra hard during and after practice. I still had to get dressed in the uniform and sit on the bench, but I wasn't going to get any minutes during games.

Paralleling my redshirt decision was my parents' unfolding decision to get divorced. The situation got realer every day until my dad finally told me it was definitely going to happen. I started crying and wondered how everything went so wrong so quickly. I talked to my mom, and she just said she didn't want to be married to him anymore.

To me, it felt like my family was being broken up. I didn't have too many friends in middle school and high school, and my parents were two people I could talk to. I had a good relationship with them and it seemed like everything was great on the outside. I was surprised by the whole thing and wished I could do something to change it. I just wanted things back to normal, but that wasn't going to happen.

One day when I went to eat with Phil in the dining hall, I wore sunglasses. The opposite of *my* situation, Phil was getting time during games and playing a lot in practices. I couldn't stop tearing up so I thought the sunglasses would help. We sat with a girl we knew and she said, "Tyson, why are you wearing sunglasses? You don't typically wear them."

I snapped back, "You don't know anything about me, how would you know what I do?"

She just looked at Phil and didn't say anything after that.

I was distraught. It was getting extremely cold in Maine, I wasn't going to be playing at all during the season, my parents were splitting up, and I was already exhausted, with a whole season full of practices still ahead of me.

Just like time doesn't stop during the happiest moments of our lives, it doesn't stop during the lowest, either. Time continues to move and we can't stop it or start it at will. Once I hit the lowest of the low, there was nothing to do but keep moving forward.

Then I started to rethink the situation. It occurred to me that one reason why I probably didn't play that well in practice was because I was getting up at 5:00 AM to get shots up before everybody else did. I looked at that and thought, *Is getting up an extra 100 shots really going to change anything?*

I decided to opt for more rest in the mornings, thinking that could translate into better mental and physical performance.

This being my first year in college basketball, I learned a lot. I observed the coaching dynamics with the players and the subtle things that occurred. A phrase we heard every day at practice was, "Last thing…"

When we heard that, the entire team felt a sense of relief that practice would be over in the next few minutes. But instead, we heard that line multiple times every practice. Sometimes, it was another half hour or even an hour before practice ended after Coach Stewart said, "Last thing…"

Eventually, we all stopped getting our hopes up.

Another thing I noticed was how hard Coach Stewart got on some of the other players. Sometimes, he'd curse them out for twenty minutes in front of everybody while the player just stood there and took it. I was glad I never got cursed out like some of them, but on the other hand, I would have liked to be a starter. So in the end would I trade getting cussed out for twenty minutes in order to play twenty minutes? Definitely.

When games officially started, I thought we were going to be the celebrities of the school. I thought I'd be able to tell people I played basketball and then; watch the awe and wonder spread across their faces. However, I realized that wasn't the case. Maine is hockey country. Instead of students camping out for tickets to our next home game, we rarely filled half the arena. But for hockey? Every game was sold out in advance.

But stepping into the opposing teams' gyms during away games made me feel like I belonged. Filing off the fancy bus and then walking into a huge gym was an experience I'd been envisioning for a long time. I felt like all the work was worth it…until the game started and I didn't play at all. But just being there gave me a sense of what was to come, and the great things I could achieve if I just put the work in.

A Day in the Life

The alarm goes off at 5:30 AM and I hit snooze. I hear it again ten minutes later as I turn it off for good. I open my eyes and sit up, my bare feet touching the cold tiles beneath me. It's still dark outside and Phil is sleeping on the other side of the room. I sit on my flimsy dorm room bed for about twenty minutes with my eyes open, but I can't move. I'm completely exhausted physically, and I start to think about what's going on right now.

I'm homesick, my parents are getting divorced, I won't be playing in any games this season, I'm getting my butt kicked during practices, and to top it all off, it's freezing cold outside with only about five hours of sunlight each day. Eventually, I reach for the pop-tart from the counter beside the bed. Some guys don't eat any breakfast, but I must have something in my stomach before I start the day. This morning it's the guards' turn to lift weights, so we'll be in the weight room for about an hour then possibly do an individual workout before class.

Once I finish the pop-tart, or as Phil calls them, Pop-Stars, I bundle up to walk out into the freezing cold. There's frost on the grass but not the cute kind of frost that rests on the top, making the green grass look like a sea of ice tips. Instead, it reminds me that nothing could survive in the deep Maine winter, and this is only the beginning.

I put on my clothes and walk outside, breathing into my jacket so the cold doesn't freeze my lungs. Finally arriving ten minutes later, the gym is dark with no signs of life. It's probably the most peace I'm going to get all day, so I embrace it.

Stopping for a moment at the gym before entering the locker room, I peek into the court through the window on the door. I smile and blow it a kiss, knowing that my hopes and dreams aren't being crushed on the court at that moment. The court looks back at me saying, "Hey man, I have nothing to do with that."

Ending my passionate moment, I walk into the locker room where, since I'm the first one there, I must turn the light on. Turning on the light gives me such a feeling of pride since I know I'm the first one to arrive. Anybody who comes in after will know there was somebody who got there first.

I change into our lifting attire as the other guys start to show up. Because it's only weight lifting, I don't feel as much pressure as I would during practice but still want to show I'm not scrawny. Once everybody gets changed, we pull out our workout sheet and walk over to the weight room.

The head trainer is already there. We share the room with other sports teams, but it's only us this morning. Typically I'd do a leg work out since the coaches want me to get my vertical jump higher, but today I'm going to pair up with another guard and do the upper body workout.

Our upper body workout consists of bench presses, triceps extensions, and back and shoulder exercises. My partner spots me as I perform the reps, then I spot him as he lifts. After about 45 minutes, we perform ab exercises: Russian twists, dead bugs, side planks, suitcases, toe touches, and bicycles.

After we all get some water and stretch, we head back to the locker room. If I knew I had a spot to play for I'd typically get some shots up, but since there's no way I will be playing in games I choose to rest up. I change and walk to class, noticing the sun as it starts to rise above the horizon.

The cold is biting so I hurry my way to the warmth of the lecture hall. The class is Economics, and I sit where I typically sit in the back right. I learn about economics for an hour then head to my next class. After that, I grab some food then finish the rest of the classes for the day.

As 3 PM hits, the sun starts to set. At first this freaked me out, but now I start to adapt and get as much sun as I can before it goes away for the night. Once classes finish, I go back to my dorm room and get ready for practice.

Every day, the anticipation of practice scares me. Since I'm the low man on the totem pole, I worry I will mess up a drill and make us redo the entire sequence again. Just the other day, I needed to make one free throw while everybody watched so we could finish practice. Because I was so nervous, I kept missing and made our team run sprints for another twenty minutes until I eventually made it.

I get to the locker room on time, hearing the normal conversation of who's banging who, who the hottest girls in the school are, or discussion about the NBA games from the previous night. When practice starts, it's the same drills that I'm getting used to. On certain drills I know I'm going to get my ass handed to me but I still continue to fight.

After a few hours of exhaustion through sprints, games and shooting drills, Coach Stewart finally says, "Last thing…" for the final time. We all huddle up, go back to the locker room, wash up, and a few of us who live together walk over to the dining hall.

In the dining hall, we continue our discussion about the NBA or who the hottest girls at Maine are. A girl walks by as I say to the guys in the tone of the voice they use, "Yooo, shorty got a bubble, B!"

Everybody cracks up. Getting beat down every day at practice isn't fun, but they knew I wouldn't quit. Because of that, I earned their respect. I began to embrace my role as the bench player and, once I accepted it, things got a lot easier.

After eating we head to the mandatory study hall where we finish any homework or papers that are due. Once finished with schoolwork, I walk back to the dorm and get some sleep, knowing tomorrow will be almost exactly the same.

--

A Few Observations

Practices

During practice we sometimes did drills where we had to box out, make a shot, or play defense a certain number of times. Until we hit that number, we continued the drill indefinitely. Since I was one of the weaker guys, I got pushed around all the time. My biggest fear was that I'd never get out of a drill.

In one drill, a coach stood at the free throw line with a player behind him, then he shot the ball. When the ball went up, the defender had to box out the offensive player then get the ball. To get out of the drill, the defender had to rebound the ball five straight times.

One time a teammate who was also struggling for playing time had to stay in a drill like this for about twenty minutes. Over and over again, the ball kept bouncing the wrong direction or he'd get four rebounds but couldn't get the fifth. Nobody was going to take it easy on him and he knew that, yet it still didn't change the fact he was exhausted. We kept pushing him until he eventually got five rebounds in a row. We all cheered for him when he got it, but we also secretly hoped that it would never happen to us.

Eventually for me, practices felt like an initiation right. I knew I was going to get beat down but I did the drills anyway. There was no way I'd back down and quit, and it's true I had always liked the challenge of playing against bigger, stronger guys. Playing with Division 1 athletes all year was going to do wonders for my game and make me a tougher player, I thought. I still had to show up though, get my ass kicked, and experience it.

College Life

Nothing against non-athletes, but I sometimes wondered what they did all day when they weren't at class. There was literally nothing else to do in the area, and even *I* got bored sometimes even with having lifting, practice, study hall, and the homework I had to do. Most classes were in lecture halls and I could tell most students weren't even listening. Instead of joining their laziness, I started to pick up on some social dynamics.

If a girl dressed up for class, I overheard other girls say, "Ugh, look at her. She's trying to look so good for everybody. What a suck up."

Other times, the same girls would say about a different girl, "Ew, that girl never dresses up. She's always in sweat pants and it's disgusting."

It seemed that no matter what other girls did, these girls would have a problem with it.

Something else I noticed was about the students who were actually invested in class. If someone was engaged, sat in the front and asked questions to the professor, you'd probably think this was the perfect student, right? Well for the students in the back of the crowd, you would have thought that person was pure evil.

They'd sarcastically say, "Oh, why don't you ask another question?" Or, "They always suck up to the teacher, what a brown-noser."

Observing this, it blew my mind. These kids were paying probably $25,000 per year to this school to learn, but instead they're just making sarcastic remarks about the kids who *do* actually want to learn and *are* interested. It made no sense to me but I didn't say anything. If anybody mentioned it, I'd just nod and say, "Yea, I know." There was no reason to get into a debate with these kids about their unproductive mindset.

Weight Lifting

During weight lifting sessions, when the head trainer wasn't around some of the guys would just slack off and talk. Even if they were better and getting more playing time than me, these guys made me sick. My mindset was that if we were in the weight room, we were there for a reason. I hated the guys who just did a few curls then chatted about the night before. To me, this was wasted time and just another example of the little things adding up in life. The universe knows when you take it easy.

In the long run, who do you think is going to benefit more: The guy who comes in to the weight room, takes it easy, and talks the whole time? Or the guy who comes in, stays focused, exerts maximum effort, and works his hardest every single rep? I would much rather go into battle with the second guy any day of the week.

--

I wasn't playing in games but it was still annoying sitting on the bench the whole time. This was Maine, so it was freezing during home games, even on the inside of the arena. We shared an arena with the hockey team so the ice below the hardwood made the place even colder than it should have been.

Since Maine is a Division 1 school, there are mandatory TV timeouts every four minutes, even if the game isn't being televised. This is the same for every Division 1 team. After every four-minute mark there's a full time out, with everybody coming to the bench to huddle. This was probably the most annoying aspect of the entire season. Since I wasn't playing all I wanted to do was sit there and cheer for my team with no interruptions. Instead, I had to stand up every four minutes, slap hands, then go back to my seat, all while freezing cold.

Whether we won or lost, I was only slightly invested in the outcome because I had no control over the game. Still, I knew the politics. If we lost, I had to look sad. If we won, I cheered and acted happy. Did I care as much as I should have? Probably not. Obviously I wanted us to win every game, but there was nothing I could do to change the outcome by warming up the end of the bench.

Phil was playing a solid amount of minutes per game, even scoring a few points once in a while. Did I get jealous that my roommate was playing twenty minutes per game while I was relegated to the practice squad? Yes. I know jealousy isn't a positive trait, but he had everything I wanted at the time. People liked him, he was scoring points and it didn't seem like he was having a rough time. He even received the Rookie of the Week Award a few times. I was happy for him, but also wished it were me.

When winter break came, the rest of the students had a few weeks off while we on the basketball team had only two days for break. I realized this was just another difference between athletes and non-athletes. I could have technically stayed home for that time since I wasn't playing in any games, but I wanted to keep practicing with the team and getting better.

When I went home for Christmas, things were very weird. My parents were separating but they were still living in the same house. My dad slept in a different room and having everybody together was just awkward. As we opened presents, they fought about insignificant things. I knew there was a lot going on beneath the surface, but there was nothing I could do or say about it. After two days, I was happy to be going back to Maine where basketball could take my mind off of it.

--

Our Christmas tournament was in Tennessee and it was cool walking through the airport together as a team. People stared at us, lots of them asking who we were. I didn't feel so bad about not playing at this point, since these people had no idea who was a starter versus who rode the bench. All they knew was that this was a basketball team with enormous players.

On road trips, we traveled in fancy busses, much like the ones from the Adidas Superstar Camp in high school. I'd never been on a road trip longer than three hours, and these trips were typically 5-8 hours long. We played teams all across the Northeast, and bus was the cheapest way to travel. One ride to Binghamton was eleven hours long, driving through the night to get there.

These first road trips were also my initiation into not having any money for food. It's now being addressed by the NCAA after Shabazz Napier from the University of Connecticut complained about starving after the championship game, but in reality it's been happening for decades. The NCAA only recently changed the rules to provide more money for athletes before and after games.

Before games, we'd have a big meal of pasta, chicken, vegetables and bread about four hours before tipoff. After the games, the coaches would literally give us $7, not a penny more. Considering most of us were broke since there was no way we could have a full time job, $7 provided little more than a small sandwich, possibly with chips. Being 6'6" athletes who pushed their bodies to the maximum every day, a small sandwich was rarely fulfilling.

When Armin brought a bag full of bagels to road trips, everybody laughed at him. But when these same guys got hungry on the bus, who do you think they went to? I know players who may or may not have stuffed as much food as they could into their bags at the dining hall before long road trips.

Another interesting aspect about road trips was how lenient the professors were with papers and grades. At times, for two straight weeks when classes were in session, we were on the road. If any papers needed to be done, we just emailed them to the professor. If at one point we needed to take a test, an administrator proctored it in the hotel room to make sure we didn't cheat. All the rules were followed when I was there, but I can only imagine what happens at larger universities where not much emphasis is placed on schooling.

Going on road trip after road trip, I learned a few things along the way:

1. If you don't want to lose anything in a hotel room, only put your stuff in one area. If you put your stuff all around the room, you may forget where you put some items.

2. Bring as much food as possible. Snacks, fruits, nuts …bring as much as you can. There will be a moment you will get hungry and instead of asking a teammate for food or spending the only $7 you have on a sandwich without chips, you will have your own supply.

3. Be a great roommate. If you snore, you can't help that, but do everything else you can. If your music is loud, turn it down. If your roommate wants the light off and you don't need it, turn it off. Clean up after yourself and make sure you don't smell too bad. You're an athlete so you're going to smell, but bring deodorant to try to control it.

4. Don't talk on your phone too loud. First, your roommate is listening to

everything and will learn a lot about you by what you say. Second, they don't want to hear you. Step outside to talk and respect the fact that somebody else is in the room.

5. Show up on time. It's easy to lie in the large, comfortable hotel beds and sleep in. If you are late there will be repercussions, even if you're not at campus.

One of the greatest things about the road trips were the moisturizers from the Marriott. Since everybody was broke, we extended the liberty of "gratuitous moisturizers." When we went back to campus, everybody smelled like the Marriott. To this day, if I smell that moisturizer somewhere, I immediately think about Phil's stack of them in the bathroom.

--

As the season progressed, we won some games and lost some games, holding onto a mediocre .500 record. Practices got easier since everybody was exhausted. The season was taking a toll on me, but mentally, things were much better. I was getting used to the life of a Division 1 basketball player and the discipline it entailed. I worked hard in the past but never worked as hard as I did in those first few months.

I started to understand the divorce and it became less of a burden. The homesickness was all but gone, since I realized I had wanted to get out of Medford for such a long time anyway. Overall, things weren't perfect, but I definitely went through a transformation over those few months.

Even though our record was mediocre, we still made the playoffs and headed to Binghamton, New York for the America East Tournament. The team who won that made it to the NCAA Tournament, and I was excited that we might have a shot. I heard if we made it in, everybody on the team got a fancy ring, which I was looking forward to.

Unfortunately, we lost our only game in the playoffs and went back to Maine the next day.

--

Once the season ended, classes went on spring break for two weeks. A few months earlier, I had set up a trip to go to the Bahamas with my dad, and now that the season was over I had the freedom to go. After the rough year I just experienced, I felt I deserved it.

Flying out, I came down from my first year playing Division 1 basketball. This was my first real vacation I'd ever been on, other than the family trips we'd taken when I was younger. Since my dad was newly single we went out to different bars each night and checked out the local scene. Some of the places were sketchy, since he insisted on going out into the "real" Bahamas, not staying in the area where they served $25 plates of pasta.

Over the vacation we discussed the divorce, the future, and what my role at Maine would be the following season. I was disappointed that I had to redshirt, but the silver lining was that I had four more years of eligibility. Four years is a long time, and that would give me ample time to build up my body, learn the system and become a great player by the time I was a senior. My dad rented a place in Philadelphia for the summer, so we agreed I'd stay there over break to work out and get ready for the following season.

When spring break ended, I went back to Maine and started the off-season workouts immediately. The trainers gave us a packet of daily and weekly workouts, which included lots of strength and conditioning exercises. In getting the packet, Olli, the 6'10" center on our team, said the previous summer he only missed one day of the workouts. At the awards banquet at the end of the season, he received the Defensive Player of the Year Award in our conference, along with First Team All-Defense. When I heard that, I made a mental note and told myself I'd follow the program to a T.

During this part of the year, I felt like I could finally take a deep breath. We still had hard workouts but they weren't as mentally, physically, or emotionally taxing as the ones earlier in the year. I adapted and realized what it took to play at this level. For the remaining two months of the semester I mainly focused on my school work.

Around this time I met Jamie, a girl who Phil introduced me to. She was also from Cameroon and it was interesting to meet someone so exotic. She spoke a few different languages, didn't know anything about basketball and had all A's in her classes. We went out a few times and she was the first girl

I really got to know since being up there.

Phil was named to the All-Rookie Team and I was proud of him, yet still a little jealous. I would have loved for that to be me, so I could shove it in Coach Adams' face back at Shawnee. It didn't happen yet, but I would be sure to get myself some minutes come the following year. Just like freshman to sophomore year in high school, I was determined to get more playing time and establish myself as an up-and-comer in the conference.

--

When school ended, I took the bus down to Philadelphia to get situated for the summer. I wasn't on such great terms with my mom, since I still didn't understand why she wanted the divorce. Regardless, there was nothing I could do about it so I just tried to accept it.

Since it was my first time living in Philly, I didn't know anybody. I was okay with this though, since my main goal was going into the next season focused and prepared. Sophomore year was always a big year and I wanted to make the most of it.

My dad helped me get an internship during the day, so I'd wake up, do a workout, then go work until 5 PM. When work finished, I'd go to the courts nearby to play streetball or do a different set of exercises from the program. Streetball in Philly was fun because there was a grittiness about the courts that was tougher than New Jersey.

I kept in contact with Coach Stewart, but I didn't get him excited about me being on the team the following season. I knew that not talking to him a lot could hurt my chances of playing time for the coming season, but I was all the way down in Philadelphia and couldn't spend the whole summer up there. A few players lived up in Maine so they'd always be around campus during the summer, getting face time with the coaches. If the coaching staff saw a player working out in the gym all summer, they would be more inclined to play them during the season because they saw that player training months before. I told the staff I was following the workout program perfectly, but since they didn't see me doing it, they had no proof. For all they knew I was watching TV all day.

Staying focused, I only missed a few days of the workout program all summer. This was my first year able to play Division 1 basketball and I hoped it would end up like Olli's the year before. I'd be in shape, I knew what I was in for, and I'd made sure to get adequate rest. There was no backup of redshirting, so I needed to be as prepared as I could to earn my spot.

--

When school started, I had a little more clout being a sophomore so I was able to get my own dorm room overlooking the gym. In terms of my redshirt eligibility, I had four years left to play but only needed three more years to graduate. If I wanted, I could use that extra year to start on a graduate degree. I could have upped my course load to possibly get a Master's Degree in five years, but didn't want to put any more pressure on myself.

When everybody on the team arrived, there were a few new faces. Phil stayed up in Maine all summer and got a lot of face time with the coaches so I knew he'd be getting a lot of minutes.

The individual workouts started almost immediately and unlike the previous season, I was prepared. I did well during practices, but still wasn't playing on the starting team. Most of the starters were juniors and seniors so I had my work cut out for me.

As practices progressed, the dust settled and it was clear who'd be playing. During scrimmages, the top five always played together to develop chemistry for the actual games, and the next five were the subs who'd battle the starters every day. Unfortunately, I wasn't even in the top ten.

It was a repeat of the year before as I was forced to watch the scrimmages. Outside of the coach's door was a newspaper article detailing the players to watch on the team, and I was nowhere to be found. I knew this was a bad sign but still clung to hope.

A few days before the games officially started, I jammed my pinkie finger on my left hand pretty bad. Phil threw me a hard pass and the middle of the pinkie bent completely backwards. I showed Coach Burden and he told me to go to the trainer. The trainer popped it back into place but I could still feel the pain. For the next few weeks, I could only play sparingly in practices, while I had to wrap up my left hand so I wouldn't re-injure it. I couldn't play as well as I wanted, and the other guys who were healthy got a lot more minutes than me.

Not knowing what to do, I thought it would be a smart idea to speak with Coach Stewart about where he saw me on the roster. Even if I wasn't going to get a huge amount of playing time, I still wanted to see where I stood on the team. After practice one day, I asked if I could discuss it with him.

In his office, I said, "I know I'm not too high on the depth chart right now, but was wondering what I could do to get more playing time."

He looked at me with a half-smile, something you'd see from a used car salesman. "Tyson, don't look at it like a depth chart. We've got a lot of great players on the team this year and we have a great chance to make it to the tournament…"

For the next twenty minutes he talked about the other players, how much potential they had and how our team could be really great. Only a few times did he actually mention me, and even then he just said we've got a lot of great freshmen. I didn't say much else after that.

When he was done talking, he smiled, shook my hand, and said, "Okay Tyson, I'll see you at practice tomorrow."

Analyzing what he told me, he didn't say anything of importance or specifics of what he wanted me to do. It was all about the other players and the team, not about how I fit into the mix. At this point, I felt my chances of getting any meaningful minutes during the season were absolutely zero.

--

Before every game, I taped up my finger and went through the warmups, hoping to get on the court for a few minutes. I wanted to be ready when my number was called, even though the chance of that was extremely low. As the games went by and I didn't get any playing time, I thought it was a joke how I taped my finger up, got ready, then took things seriously. The other players probably thought it was comical that I thought I'd get any playing time. Regardless, I took it seriously because that's what I always did with basketball.

When Christmas came around I had played a total of five minutes all season. They were trash minutes, provided at the end of a blowout win against a Division 3 school. On the court for those few minutes, I shot the ball every time I touched it.

Coach Stewart yelled at me on the sideline during that game, "Tyson, there are other players on the court! Pass the ball!"

I thought, *You fucker. These are the only minutes you're going to giving me all year and now you want me to pass the ball? I don't think so.*

The epitome of the season came in January when we traveled to New Jersey for a game against the New Jersey Institute of Technology in Newark. They just came up to the Division 1 level from Division 2 and still hadn't won a game at the Division 1 level yet. I thought it was the perfect time to get some minutes and show that I deserved to be on the court.

Since it was close to home, my mom, sister and her friend all came to the game. They were excited to see me play since they hadn't seen me in a long time. One of my ex-teammates from my sixth grade travel team was on NJIT, so it was a homecoming of sorts. I was in New Jersey, my family was there, and I'd be playing against a guy I grew up with.

The game started and I didn't play at all in the first half. That was fine, I thought, since we wanted to get a lead on them before the bench players came in. With about ten minutes left in the game, I still hadn't played and we were up by about twenty points. As the clock ticked down, I started to get nervous since I knew it would take me a minute or two to get warmed up.

With five minutes left, the game was easily out of reach for NJIT. I still hadn't played one second though. I was getting angry, realizing the clock was slowly ticking away. Eventually, the clock ticked down to zero. I didn't get in the game for even one second. The other guys were happy because we won, but I was pissed off.

We walked over and shook the hands of NJIT as I said hi to my former teammate. It was cool seeing him again, and how our lives converged after all these years. He probably wondered why I didn't play at all, as I was wondering the same thing.

My mom, sister, and her friend walked over. They were also confused, curious as to why I didn't play when the game was clearly out of reach. My mom, typically calm, was angry. She said she spoke with Coach Stewart briefly at halftime, and he told her I was doing great in practices and how I was such an integral part of the team.

If Stewart put me in the game, I had ability. It's not like NJIT would immediately score twenty points the second I got onto the court. I knew what I was doing and I was an asset. The fact that he didn't play me one second in that game showed me the real character of who he was, behind all his smiles and bullshit encouragement.

After the game I asked Coach Burden why I didn't play, and he just said, "I don't know man, I don't control playing time."

Traveling back to Maine, I felt sick about the whole situation. Here I was, shooting around 300 shots per day after practice, doing everything right, and starting to play well during scrimmages. I wasn't the best player, but I knew I could hit some shots when I got the ball and be trusted to make the right decisions.

Every four minutes during games, I stood up, walked over to the huddle then walked back down to my seat on the bench. I put on the uniform, warmed up with the team, and cheered all throughout the games. I was supportive of the players and rebounded for the starters in warmups.

All of it seemed to me like an exercise in futility. It felt like wasted time, energy, and talent, being at the end of the bench when I knew I could play with this team if I just got the chance. All I needed was a chance, but I didn't get it.

One of the final games of the season was a home game and I still had a sliver of hope I could play. Before our team warmed up, I went to the court and got extra shots up to be ready just in case. The team was particularly bad so I was hoping I could get onto the court for a few minutes during the game.

With about ten minutes remaining in the match, we had a twenty point lead. Bundling up in the cold gym, I just sat there realizing I probably wasn't going to play during this game, either.

I saw Coach Stewart look down the bench and my eyes briefly locked his. Hoping he would shout my name, he instead turned his head back to the game and sat down. About a minute later, I heard, "Tyson, get in!"

I lifted my head but thought my teammates were just messing with me. Stewart stood up and looked at me again saying, "Tyson!"

Realizing this wasn't just an auditory mirage, I stood up and ran to the scorer's table as my teammates started cheering for me. Once the crowd saw me run to the table, they started cheering too, since they loved to see the bench players get some minutes.

Arriving at the scorer's table, I told them my plans to check in. They smiled and gave me the thumbs up sign. I thought, *This is it! I'm going to play with ten minutes left in the game!*

I took off my warmup and threw it to the side. I stood there watching the plays, getting ready to check in once the ball went out of bounds. Right before I was about to check in, I looked down in shock.

I had forgotten to put my jersey on.

There were a few gasps from the fans and I didn't know what to do. I was wearing a white spandex shirt that we wore under our jerseys, so fortunately I wasn't shirtless. Some people started laughing since I couldn't check into the game without a jersey. This wasn't streetball, this was an official NCAA event.

Coach Stewart looked disappointed and told me to go get my jersey. I ran past the bench to the locker room to get it from my locker. But when I got to the locker room door, it was locked. I thought, *Oh, this is wonderful.*

I went back out in my spandex shirt to get the trainer, who had the key for the locker room. I dug out my jersey, put it on and ran back to the court to check into the game.

Since there were only about five minutes left at this point, I took a few shots and it still felt great to be on the court. I was pissed at myself for not remembering to put my jersey on, but thought, *Who cares*.

What happened was that since I warmed up before the official warmups, there was no reason to put on the jersey. When I got back into the locker room, I got caught up in everything and only put my warmup on.

A few of the guys made fun of me after the game for it, and I just laughed along with them. It wasn't a serious game and meant nothing in terms of how much court time I'd see in the future, or at least that's what I hoped. It was just an embarrassing moment for a bench player who never got into the game.

--

The season finished the same way as the year before, with us traveling to the America East tournament only to lose in the first game. That was fine with me, since this season was another disaster in terms of playing time. I was looking forward to hitting the reset button again.

It wasn't the ideal year for me, but it was better than nothing. I got experience on the team and scored some points during the games. I practiced all year and knew I was definitely improving. Division 1 ball was tough but I was getting used to it. I still had three more years of eligibility, so I was looking forward to developing into one of the best players in the conference.

At the end of every season, players have interviews with the coaches to figure out what happened during the season and what the game plan is for the summer going into the following year. They're not very formal, but it's possible to learn a lot about where you stand on the team during these discussions. When it was my turn for the interview, I went into Coach Stewart's office.

Entering the room, the sun was shining through the office window behind him. He sat behind a huge desk with basketball books and DVD's in the cabinet to the right. Scouting reports lined his desk and ran onto the floor beside us. We started talking to recap the past year, and I told him I felt I was improving and getting more comfortable with the system. I felt he screwed me over a few times, but in talking to him I took the high road and was willing to put that behind us to set myself up for the following season.

About halfway through our conversation, he spoke the words that altered my trajectory in life forever.

He said, "Tyson, you will never play at this school."

Confused, I replied, "Um, what do you mean?"

He continued, "Here's the deal. You can be on the team, but you will never get any significant playing time. I honored the scholarship that Coach Gianinni gave you, but you will be a practice player here until you graduate. Now, I don't know if that's what you want, but that's the reality of your situation."

His words hit me like a ton of bricks and I must have looked like a deer in headlights. Here I was, ready to work my butt off for him this summer and do whatever he asked, but instead, he had other plans for me. These plans turned out to be no plans at all.

I tried to bargain with him, telling him I thought I was as good as some of the other starters. "I can be an asset if I get some more playing time since I'm really starting to learn the system."

"Tyson, we're bringing in a lot of great players next year, and you're not going to have a shot against them."

I knew I could hang with anybody, but there was nothing I could say to change his mind.

"Look, Tyson, lots of players do it. They'll go to a Division 1 school, then transfer to a lower level school like a Division 3."

I thought, *I would never do that. My goal was to play Division 1 basketball, not Division 3.*

For the rest of the conversation, I just stared at his pasty face as he told me how great the team was going to be the following year. I was in a daze, wondering what the hell was happening. I thought, *Do I want to keep my scholarship and be a bench player for the next three years? Or do I want to get the hell out of Maine and get playing time somewhere else?*

Once he stopped talking, we shook hands and I walked out of his office. After that, my first order of business was to call Rick and explain to him the situation.

Rick picked up, "What's up Big Tymerrrrr?"

"Rick, I just had my exit interview with Coach Stewart and he told me I would never play at Maine. He told me those exact words."

He got serious, "Okay, I'll call some coaches in Philly right now and tell them. I know a few guys who would love to have you on their team."

We talked for a little longer and since he knew this was tough for me, he didn't give me any shit about it. I walked out of the gym and into the sunlight with absolutely no idea of what to do next.

--

Back at my dorm, I called my dad and told him the situation, too. He asked what I wanted to do and I said I still didn't know yet.

I then called Jamie, my girlfriend, and told her. She said, "Well, you're going to stay here, right?"

I responded, "Most likely, but I really want to play. I don't just want to sit the bench for the next few years."

She replied, "Yea, but you can play during practices. You don't *have* to play during the games. They're giving you a scholarship and that's the most important thing, it doesn't matter if you play or not."

Thinking that was the weirdest sentence I'd ever heard, I agreed with her anyway. Stewart said something else in the meeting about most college romances not lasting a year or two since he knew I was with Jamie. When he said that, I thought, *No way. I really like Jamie and there's no way we'd break up. We're stronger than that.*

Over the next few weeks, I thought about what I should do. One day I was in my car and I started punching the dashboard over and over. For twenty minutes, I screamed and hit anything I could until I knocked a drink onto the floor. I got a paper towel to clean it up, and took a deep breath. I told myself, "Getting angry isn't going to do anything about this, so calm your emotions, and figure out what you're going to do."

I was still working out with the team until the school year ended and some of the teammates knew my situation. I tried to determine my future by seeing how I felt during workouts. I'd think, *Okay, let's say that I stay,* and tried to see if I felt better during sprints. When I thought about playing Division 3, I actually ran faster and it felt better. Even though I wanted to play four years at a Division 1 school, I realized it was now highly unlikely.

After hours of discussions with Rick, my parents, Jamie and Coach Burden, I decided to leave Maine. The major factor in my decision was that I just didn't want to be a bench player for the next two years, standing up and sitting down every four minutes during my prime years of college. The second major factor was pride. I knew I was a good player. When my teammates and the fans saw me sitting on the bench during games, they probably thought of me as a scrub. I knew I was good; I just hadn't gotten the chance to prove myself.

I didn't want to just put on a jersey every game, warm up with the team, and know I wasn't going to play one minute. I wanted to put my talent and skills to good use, not just clap for the team when they did well and look sad when they lost. I wanted to be truly invested in the team and have genuine emotions whether we won or lost.

With Jamie, we both decided we'd try to make it work. I told her I was going down to Medford for a while to figure out what my next steps would be. Since I wasn't on scholarship anymore, the team wasn't going to pay for me to stay up in Maine.

The weekend after school ended, I packed my stuff into the Chevy Blazer my dad helped me get a few months earlier, ready to drive back down to Medford. Before I left, Coach Burden called me and said, "Are you sure this is what you want to do? There's no turning back from here. We're going to start recruiting new players and give up your room."

Resigned to the circumstances, I replied, "Yea…I'm sure."

There's a saying that goes, "Basketball is a business." When I initially heard that saying, I thought, *No, basketball is a sport, not a business.*

When Coach Burden said that final line to me though, I understood exactly what the saying meant. The coaching staff may have cared about me, but at the end of the day I was still just a tool for the team. When they didn't need this tool anymore, they just brought in a different tool that would help the team accomplish their perpetual pursuit of wins. Once I stopped playing basketball for them, I wasn't an asset anymore, and there was no use for me.

I was worthless.

4
THE DARK TIMES

My sister was living with my mom in Medford and my dad was now in New York. I wasn't on the best terms with my dad since he didn't like Jamie. Also, because I was nearly broke, I kept asking him for money.

Jamie suggested I get some loans to have money to help her pay for things. Since I thought we were in love and she never had money, I bought her clothes and even helped her buy a car. I got one or two credit cards, as well as a $5,000 loan from Sallie Mae since my credit was perfect at the time. At Bank of America when I was applying for a credit card, I told the lady it was to buy a car.

She said, "Oh what kind?"

Lying to her, I thought of the first brand that came into my mind, "Honda."

She replied, "Oh, that's a great brand," as I hoped she didn't pry with any more questions.

Getting the $5,000 from Sallie Mae at Jamie's urging, I had some money for a few months. I told my mom I'd be driving down there one night as she told me to let myself in.

Back at the house, it felt weird being there again. I stared at the hoop that I trained at for years and years to play Varsity and get my scholarship. After everything I'd experienced, here I was, back home, with no idea of what to do next.

I entered the house and slept in the guest room, since it was too weird to sleep in the same bed I grew up in. When my mom and sister woke up the next day, we all gave each other hugs, but they were busy so they couldn't spend too much time with me.

When they left for the day, I felt like a complete failure. Years of hard work to get my Division 1 scholarship had all been for nothing. I was hoping to play four years at a Division 1 school, get drafted to the NBA or play overseas, then live the good life after that. Now, I had screwed it all up.

Rick told me I wouldn't be able to play at another Division 1 school since Maine wasn't that good, and no team would pick me up if I couldn't even play there. My only option was to play at a lower level like Division 2 or 3, but I didn't want to be seen as a Division 3 player.

Another feeling that weighed on me was just feeling sick of basketball. Before college, I liked to run, have freedom, and play my game. But the years at Maine sucked the passion out of me. Instead of basketball being a sport, it felt like a business. We trained in the morning, did the drills, then went home. The coaches dictated our role, and if we skewed from that at all, we could be kicked off the team. All the love I had for the game was gone.

I was lost. I had no direction and no idea of what to do next. For the past six years, my only goal was to play and thrive at a Division 1 school. That was now all over and I felt like a complete failure.

The weekend came and I was utterly depressed. I didn't show it on the outside, but my mind was fucked. I had no backup plan, and I felt like I had no future.

On Friday, I told my mom I was going to Craig's house for the weekend. I needed to get out of Medford since I was losing my mind there. Instead of going to Craig's though, I got on the highway and drove east towards the beach.

A friend picked me up a twelve pack of Budweiser as I cruised toward the ocean. On the drive, everything hit me. I was a failure. Once everybody heard about how I was leaving Maine, they'd probably think I was a loser. I felt that nobody understood me and nothing could make this better. I had no future and there was nothing that would make me happy. My life was worthless, so I had no choice but to end it all.

--

On my way east, I was thinking of ways how I would end my own life. I stopped at a Dick's and asked the guy if I could check out one of the guns behind the counter. He was an older, weathered guy, and he just stared me up and down.

He looked at me straight in the eye and said, "You can't touch one of these unless you have a valid permit."

I replied, "Okay, no problem," while I looked around at other stuff in the store. There was an area with knives and I bought one.

Back in the car, I was wondering where I should end it all. I opened the knife and stuck it into my stomach a little bit. I thought, *Shit, that hurts.* I closed the knife back up and kept driving to the shore.

I took the highway all the way down and ended up in Long Beach Island. This is where many of the kids from Shawnee would talk about having vacation houses, and where they went on the weekends. I'd never been there except for a class trip in eighth grade at Moorestown Friends to study the coastline.

It got dark, and I didn't know where I was going to sleep. I parked along the coast somewhere, starting to drink some of the beers. I got out and walked along the beach near the big lighthouse. Some couples walked by and I thought of the difference between our lives. Here they were, happy people walking along the beach, while I was just looking for an area to off myself.

I walked along the beach for a while in a daze. As the beers kicked in I headed back to the Chevy Blazer. I drove around and finally found a spot near a house under some trees where I figured nobody would see the car or question me. I put my head back and slept in the car that night.

The next day, the depression hit me even harder. I felt even more worthless than the day before. I started drinking early, even more determined to off myself that day. Nobody was calling me on my phone, which showed that nobody even gave a shit about me.

I got some food at a sandwich shop then saw a fishing store nearby. I walked in and looked around, finding a huge knife with a long blade, typically used for opening fish. Since I didn't want it to look suspicious I was only buying a huge knife, I bought some lures as well.

The lady at the checkout said, "Oh, those are perfect for the blue gills today!"

I responded, "Yea, I know, thanks a lot."

Since the stabbing earlier had hurt, I figured I would choose another way to end my life. I went to a sporting goods store and found some duct tape and tennis balls. The plan was to tape a ball to the exhaust pipe of the car, so the fumes would end my life peacefully. To complement this plan, I'd take a whole bunch of sleeping pills to be unconscious as it happened.

I stopped at the drug store to pick up a bunch of pills. I went back to the place I slept the night before and taped up a tennis ball to the exhaust of the car. I then got into the driver's seat and opened the bottle of pills. I texted a few people, telling them I was sorry and I loved them, and it wasn't their fault. I don't think the texts went through though, since I didn't have service.

Before I took the pills, I had a moment of doubt. I thought, *Maybe there was a reason for my life? Maybe I should live?* The thought of life flashed briefly, but then I realized what a stupid idea that was. I was worthless and a failure. I took out about eight of the sleeping pills, put them into my mouth, and swallowed. I added six ibuprofens and figured that would do the trick. Combine that with the tennis ball on the exhaust and I was bound to succeed.

I laid back, closed my eyes, and went to sleep.

--

I woke up about an hour later wondering where I was. The car was shaking and it was extremely hot since all the windows were up. I opened the door and checked on the exhaust pipe, which was shaking. The tennis ball was working, but some fumes were still escaping through the duct tape. I was pissed off and figured this wasn't going to work. I ripped off the tape and removed the tennis ball. I got back in the car and drove to a different spot, since I felt like somebody might arrive at that house soon.

Night approached as I finished the rest of the beer. I decided I needed to take more direct action. I parked the car in a secluded area and hid the knife in my pants as I walked to the edge of the ocean. I thought ending my life on a beach would be poetic, so that was the goal.

The sky was dark and nobody was around. Drunk from the beer and pills, I figured now would be the perfect time to meet my maker. I laid back on the soft sand as I took the knife to my wrists. A few minutes passed and nothing happened, so I realized this wasn't going to work either.

I was a failure... again.

I didn't want anybody to walk up on me, so I went back to the car and put a sweatshirt over my head. I tried to sleep but it was impossible. Eventually I just wanted to get back home so I started the drive back to Medford. I passed the house where I slept outside the night before and saw a car in the spot where I was parked. I was glad I had moved my car.

Driving west, I wasn't exactly sure how to get back to Medford. My phone battery died and I couldn't contact anybody. After about thirty minutes, I took an exit and found an area near a lake. Nobody was around so I parked the car, put my head back, and went to sleep.

--

The sun woke me up the next morning and I actually felt a little better. I didn't accomplish what I wanted to at the beach, but figured there was a reason for it. I thought, *God's keeping me around for some reason.* I contemplated trying it again, but figured I'd just fail again.

Both my contacts had fallen out the night before so I was nearly blind. I headed to the highway again and squinted whenever I couldn't see anything. After about an hour I found some familiar signs and got on the right road back to Medford. Just before I made it back to the house, I tried to clean myself up a bit.

When I pulled into the driveway, my mom immediately ran out. She came up and gave me a huge hug, practically crying and asking where I was. I told her I was at Craig's house.

She said, "I called Craig and he said had no idea where you were."

I replied, "Okay, well whatever."

She said she called everybody, including Rick, and nobody had any idea where I was.

I said, "Well I'm here now, so there's no need to worry." I went into the house and called a few people who knew I was missing.

When I talked to Rick, he said, "You were with another girl, weren't you?"

I laughed and said, "Nah man."

He said, "Ohh yea you were, hahaha!" I just laughed with him, wishing that's all it was.

Now that I was back in Medford, I had to actually plan out what to do with my life. After everything that just happened, I figured I needed to find a therapist to help me through this. I looked online and there was a psychiatrist that dealt with depression right down the street. I booked an appointment with her the next day. There was a $40 co-pay to see her, but I needed the help more than I needed that $40.

I walked into her room and saw a middle-aged lady with brown hair. I sat down and we started talking. She asked what the problem was as I told her the broad strokes of my situation. I didn't get into detail, but told her about the basketball team and how I didn't know what was next for my life.

She asked, "Have you ever attempted suicide or do you have suicidal thoughts?"

Not wanting her to think I was a freak or send me to a hospital, I replied, "No, I just can't think, and I feel lost."

When we finished talking, she said the problem was that the neurons in my brain weren't firing correctly. She provided me with a few pills and a prescription for an antidepressant drug.

I asked, "So that's it, just take the pills and everything will be better?"

She replied, "Yea, just make sure you take them consistently. It may take two weeks for them to kick in, but they'll correct the brain chemistry."

I walked out of her office certain she'd just robbed me of my $40 co-pay. I thought, *Ok, so I just take a few pills and that'll change everything about my situation? I don't think so lady.*

I took the dose she recommended but nothing changed. I slept on the couch that night and in the morning I woke up to the sun's rays beating down on me. I felt refreshed and thought, *Maybe the pills* are *starting to work.* I didn't want to get addicted to them though, so I didn't take any more. I wanted things to happen naturally, not needing the crutch of antidepressants.

Since I did feel a little better, I started to think about what to do next. One thing was for certain: I was finished with basketball. The seasons were too intense and it made me lose my passion for the game. At the college level, they just treated me like a tool, not letting me play my game. There was no leeway and no freedom.

I told everybody my decision and they all supported me. In their eyes, I was too focused on basketball anyway, so it'd be good for me to open my eyes to new experiences. For the past ten years of my life, my only focus was on playing basketball. I wanted the scholarship so bad that nothing else mattered. Since that experience was now over, I had a chance to re-establish myself as a new person and start to live a normal life. Everybody thought it was great for me, but I was nervous about it. Without basketball I didn't know what to do.

I definitely didn't want to live in Medford, so I looked for jobs in New York City. The goal was to maybe take a year off and just work while I planned my next steps. Searching online for jobs, I found one saying that the base pay was $17 an hour, plus commission. It seemed interesting, so I applied and got an interview.

I took the bus up to New York and did the interview. It was a group interview at first, where they asked us typical questions and explained the job, which was selling knives. They sold me on the position and I agreed to work for them. I had a job, now I just needed a place to live.

I went onto Craigslist and checked out apartments to sublet. There was a place for about $1,600 a month on the Upper West Side that I thought was perfect. It was a small room but it had a bed and a bathroom, which was all I needed. The plan was to only stay there for a few months until I figured out what I wanted to do for the school year. My mom gave me money to help with the security deposit, and I signed the sublet for the room.

In my mind, things were looking up. I had a job, I had a place to live, and I didn't have to play basketball anymore. I could just focus on making money and living a normal life.

--

When I arrived at the new hire orientation for the job, they packed about thirty of us into a room. We walked through the sales process and they told us to write down every person we had ever met in our entire lives. The loud, outspoken guy in the front of the room explained that the people who had the most names on their list sold the most knives. When I wrote down my names, I finished with about 600. The guy then told us to get in contact with those people and set up appointments to sell the knives.

We were provided with a script of what to say and once I started calling, it actually worked. I set appointments, sat down with people in their homes, then performed the sales process of why they should buy the knives. It was kind of weird, but I needed the money so I did it anyway.

When I talked to the people who knew I played basketball, their biggest question for me was if I was going to play again. Over and over again, I explained that I was finished with it and just wanted to live a normal life.

I sold a lot of knives in the first few weeks, thanks to a huge order I got from my Aunt Shauna. After her purchase though, nobody else bought a significant amount. I found it uncomfortable trying to pitch a person I didn't know something they didn't need. Once I got past close family and friends, I didn't want to sit in a strange person's house and try to sell them knives. It did help me with my sales skills though, and I learned a lot.

Since I wasn't making money with the knives, I wasn't able to pay for the apartment. I told the girl who rented it out to me that I wouldn't be able to pay, and she told me to find someone else to cover it for the remaining months. I went on Craigslist and quickly found someone.

Jamie and I were still together and we agreed that living together up in Maine would be good for our relationship. One weekend, I packed up the Blazer and drove my way from New York City to Augusta, Maine.

There, she was gone for most of the day while I applied for different jobs. Eventually, I got a job through a temp agency doing data entry right down the street from the apartment. I had no path, purpose, or focus, just the knowledge that I needed to work somewhere to make a few dollars.

We lived together for the summer, but I still didn't know what I was going to do in the fall. I thought I might attend Rutgers University as a student without playing basketball, but wasn't sure. At the end of the summer though, the universe made its decision for me.

Jamie's internship wrapped up and she went back to Orono, about an hour from Augusta. It was my last week of the data entry job, and the plan was for me to commute from Orono to Augusta for the final week since her sublet finished for the summer.

I always took care of the Blazer, even though the check engine light went on sometimes. One day though, as I was driving back to Orono after work, the Blazer started to slow down on the highway. I tried to put pressure on the gas, but it kept slowing and the steering wheel didn't turn. I pumped the brakes as the SUV slowed to a stop on the side of the road. I tried to turn the ignition but nothing happened.

I called Jamie and told her, but she said she couldn't come down until the weekend. I told her it was an emergency but she still said there was nothing she could do. There was no way I could get into her apartment since it was all locked up. I called a tow truck and they took the car to an auto shop nearby. The day was nearly over, but the guy told me he could take a look at it in the morning. I didn't want to spend money on a taxi and hotel so I just bundled up and slept in the car that night.

This was the middle of the week, so I still had to go to work. In the morning, I walked there from the auto shop at 6 AM. As I was trudging down the highway in the freezing cold Maine morning, I wondered what the heck I was doing.

I did this for the next few nights until the week finished up. On the last day of the week, I told my parents what was happening and they helped me get a hotel.

I called my mom and she said, "Tyson, come home."

Hearing that, I knew it was the only thing to do. There was nothing for me up in Maine, I was technically homeless, and the Blazer was shot so I didn't even have a car. It seemed like Jamie didn't really care if I was there or not, so that weekend I booked a Greyhound ticket to come back to Medford once and for all.

--

My mom picked me up from the Greyhound station in Marlton and drove me back to the house. It was now September and my sister had gone off for her freshman year of college at St. Joseph's University in Philadelphia. She left the car we used in high school in the driveway, a Volkswagen Passat. Contemplating what I should do, I started looking for jobs in the area again. There was an opening for a salesperson at Burlington Coat Factory, and with my knife-selling experience I thought I'd be a good fit.

I did well during the interview, especially when I told them, "I understand the power of a team." A few days after, they called me back and told me I was hired. I began my stint as a "Suit Specialist," working about thirty hours per week selling suits to men who came into the section to browse. It wasn't the most important job in the world, but it was something.

My 21st birthday rolled around on September 17th, 2007. Most of my friends were still off at college, with Gil being the only person from the neighborhood still around. He was the one who helped ease my transition into Medford six years before and was truly a good friend. He didn't see me as a failure since I had quit basketball at Maine, he just saw me as a friend who was now back in Medford.

A few days before my 21st birthday, I lost my ID somewhere so there was no way I'd be able to get into any bars. While the typical 21st birthday for someone consisted of going out with a group of friends and getting wasted, I instead sat in my living room with Gil as we watched something on TV. I chalked it up to being different.

--

Even though I was working about forty hours per week at Burlington Coat Factory, I was still broke. Because I didn't have any money, I constantly received overdraft notices from Bank of America, stating I owed them $35 for going into the negative. At the grocery store, I'd load up on pasta since that was the cheapest food that filled me up. I went to the Wawa one day with only 83 cents to my name. I bought a pack of cookies. The cookies were only 63 cents and I used my debit card, hoping nobody would question why I used my card for a 63-cent purchase.

Jamie always wanted me to send her money, and I obliged since I thought that's what boyfriends did. If I didn't, she'd get mad at me or try to justify why I should send her a certain amount.

On November 27th, right after Thanksgiving, Jamie told me she wanted to break up. I thought she was homesick or just missing me so I deflected the statement. I told her I'd call her more or possibly even go up there to visit. She said none of those things mattered. I didn't make her happy anymore and the long distance relationship wasn't working out.

Hearing this, it woke me up because I really believed we were in love. I didn't know why she'd say something like this, and the rest of the conversation was me pleading with her to change her mind. However, at the end, she said she had made up her mind.

For me, this changed everything. She'd been there with me through the ups and downs of playing Division 1 basketball at Maine, yet now here I was, living in my mom's basement and working a minimum wage job in Medford, New Jersey. There's no way this was what she wanted in a guy. Honestly, I couldn't blame her, but I was going to do everything I could to get her back.

On a Friday night after I got paid, I cashed my check and drove to the entrance of the Jersey Turnpike. I thought, *Tyson, do you really want to do this?* I answered my question by turning on Kanye West's "Stronger" and heading north. I hoped the Passat could handle the ride, because I was about to drive ten hours through the night to Orono, Maine.

Arriving in Maine the next morning, I called Jamie and told her I was in town. She thought I was lying, just saying that so we could talk on the phone longer. When I pushed and told her I was actually there, she said she was going into class but could see me afterward. I hung around Orono for a few hours, reminiscing of the places I went when I was on the team and excited to be playing basketball at a Division 1 school. Now, I had no plan for my life, quit basketball, and was desperately trying to see the girl who broke up with me.

It was pathetic.

When we met, I told her that I loved her and still wanted to be with her. She told me the distance was taking its toll, and there was no way we could be together if I was going to stay in Jersey. I told her we could try to make it work but she wasn't interested.

There was nothing else I could do or say so I just gave her a hug, got in the Passat, and started the drive back down to Medford. On the highway back down, a cop stopped me because the tags on the Passat were expired.

He inquired, "Where are you coming from?"

I replied, "You don't want to know."

He went back to his vehicle to check the license plate, then came back and asked again. This time, I told him I drove up to Maine to see a girl and I was now driving back down.

For a second he held a silent pause, which implied, "Damn."

--

In Medford, the effects of the breakup were overwhelming. I felt like I lost a part of myself and it hurt every night. Going into the job at Burlington Coat Factory, I'd cry sometimes on my way to work, then compose myself right before my shift to sell some suits. After work, I'd try to drink some beer to dampen the sting, but nothing helped. One night, I asked, "God, please have it not hurt that much tonight." That night, it was a little better. I looked at myself in the mirror one day and was appalled at how skinny I'd become.

I realized sitting in the house and sulking wasn't going to help, so I needed something to get my mind off the breakup. I called my uncle in Chicago and he said I could come out there for a few days. I'd spend Christmas with my mom, sister, and grandma in Medford, but getting out of Jersey for a few days before the 25th would really help.

In Chicago, it felt good to spend time with family, but the effects of the breakup still lingered. At the airport in Philadelphia after the trip, I felt completely lost again. I emailed my aunt from Chicago whom I just saw, writing, "I just feel completely lost and have no idea what to do."

Fortunately, she immediately responded with some words of encouragement. I was fighting dark thoughts, but it was a tough fight. I'd been down that road once before and I didn't want to go back.

There was a sheet I printed out about the meaning of indifference. I had never understood what it meant until then, but I was trying to get to the point where I neither loved nor hated Jamie, just felt indifference towards her. I tried and tried but it was mighty hard.

Christmas Day arrived and I spent it with my sister, grandma, and mom. We opened presents and listened to Christmas music. It felt good and helped ease the sting of Jamie.

In the afternoon, I got bored so I went outside to shoot baskets in the driveway. In between shots, I saw Gil's sister walk by, coming up from the path that led to the lake. I waved to her and she waved back, but I could tell she was crying. I walked over to her and said, "Hey, what's wrong?"

Her eyes were puffy as she looked up at me and said, "Gil's gone."

"Oh, where'd he go?"

"He died last night."

Confused, I asked, "What do you mean? I just saw him a few weeks ago.

What are you talking about?"

"The police are labeling it a suicide and they said drugs were involved."

Shocked and confused, I started to cry and gave her a big hug. I thought, *Is she serious? Is this real?*

I asked her again and again if she was sure and she kept saying yes. Gil was probably my best friend at that point, someone who helped me when I came to Medford and truly supported me over the previous months.

A day later, Gil's parents called my mom and told her what happened. They said drugs were involved and the police took his laptop to investigate. My mom and I were both distraught, and I called my dad up in New York City to tell him the news. I asked if I could stay with him for a few days to get my mind off of it and he agreed.

The next day, I took the Greyhound up to New York.

--

My dad and I spent a few days together while I tried to figure out what my next steps would be. I quit the job at Burlington Coat Factory right before Christmas since I was planning to go to college in the coming semester. I still didn't know where I wanted to attend, but knew I didn't want to be trapped working that job for forty hours a week.

After a few days in New York, I had to get out. I was still talking to Jamie sporadically, even though we weren't technically together. Deep down, I still wanted her back, and thought going up to Maine again would be the best way to accomplish this. I went to the bus station and booked a ticket to Bangor.

Standing in line waiting for the bus, I noticed a girl ahead of me who looked like one of Jamie's friends. I said her name and she turned around.

She looked at me and said, "Tyson?!"

I said, "Hey, how you doing? Are you going back to Maine?"

"Yea, I am. Are you?"

"Yea, I'm going too."

"Oh, nice! What are you going up there for?"

"Well honestly, I want to surprise Jamie."

She hesitated, "I thought you guys weren't together anymore…"

"Yea we're not, but I want to see her and talk to her in person."

"Oh, okay. That's cool."

We talked a little more and got onto the bus when it arrived. Seeing her here, it seemed that God definitely wanted me to go back to Maine.

--

When we arrived in Orono, I showed up with Jamie's friend at her apartment. The expression on her face said, "What the hell are you doing here?"

She brought her friend inside the apartment but told me to wait outside since she had family over. When she came out, I told her what was going on and why I was there. She was sympathetic about Gil, but said that didn't mean we could still be together. At the end, she asked me what I was going to do next.

I said, "I guess I'll just head back to New York."

"I think that's a good idea."

She let me sleep on the floor of her apartment that night then took me to the Greyhound station the next day. I heard that stupid Sean Kingston song, "She got me suicidaaaalllll, suicidaaaalllll," play on the radio as I tried to not take it as a sign.

It was dark as the bus approached the Boston bus terminal. I didn't want to go back to New York since I felt I was being a burden on my dad. Medford wasn't an option because I couldn't deal with the Gil situation. I felt like nobody cared what was happening, since nobody was texting or calling me. I thought the Sean Kingston song from earlier in the day was a sign, and God finally wanted me to end my life for good.

I walked around the bus station trying to find the best way to end my life. I thought, *Should I walk into an oncoming train? Should I get some police officers to shoot at me? Should I go to the top of a high-rise and jump off?*

After a half hour, I wasn't sure which would be the best course of action but I continued the deliberation. While weighing my options, I figured telling one or two people before I acted would be polite. It'd be a courtesy call of sorts so they wouldn't be surprised.

First, I called my sister. When she picked up, she said, "Hey Tys, what's up?!"

"Nothing much, how you doing?"

"Nothing, just hanging out."

"Cool."

Summoning the courage to tell her what was about to happen, I just said it, "Ali, I love you, but I'm finished with my life. I'm sick of everything, and there's no purpose for me at all anymore."

There was a silence. Then she said, "What?? What are you talking about??!!"

"There's no reason for me to be alive in this world anymore. I love you and you can keep all my stuff. Bye Ali."

She started freaking out and crying, but I just hung up. There was nothing more to say, and I didn't want to hear her try to reason me out of it when I felt it was what I was destined to do. I almost threw my phone in the trash so I wouldn't have to hear from anybody else, but I thought that'd be suspicious if anybody saw it. Instead, I hung onto the phone while I contemplated my next steps.

A minute later, my phone started ringing. The caller ID said it was my dad, and I figured I'd tell him what was going to happen, too.

I picked up, "Hey man."

My dad casually said, "Hey, how you doing?"

"Good."

"Ok, well Ali just called me hysterically crying, telling me you said there's no reason for your life anymore, and that she could keep all your stuff."

Getting angry she would tell him, I replied, "What, are you going to give me shit for it??!! You don't really care if I'm here or not anyway!"

He calmly said, "No, I just want to know what's going on. What's wrong?"

I took a deep breath and spilled everything out to him. I told him I was in Boston after heading up to Maine to see Jamie for the weekend, and how I felt I had no direction or purpose for my life. He didn't say anything… he just listened. After five minutes of talking, I knew I wasn't going to try to off myself anymore. In reality, I just needed someone to talk to and someone who cared.

We talked for the next ten minutes. As the conversation winded down, he said he'd get me a hotel down the street for the night. I agreed to that and he said my Uncle Mike would be calling me soon, too. I hung up and waited for the call from my uncle. Talking to him, I could tell he had no idea what to say, but it was just nice to talk to someone who cared. After I spoke with him, Phil called me.

In his thick accent, he said, "Hey man, what you doing, huh? What's going on mannn?"

Remembering his funny accent, I started laughing. "I'll be okay, man, don't worry."

After Phil, I talked to my mom for a few minutes, and even Jamie called since Phil told her what was going on. Even if I looked like an idiot, it was still nice to talk to everybody.

A half hour after I initially called my sister, my dad called back and told me they reserved me a hotel room within walking distance from the bus station. The lady at the reception desk greeted me with a smile. I took the elevator up to the room and walked in.

Two minutes later, I heard a knock on the door. I opened it and saw a huge police officer staring at me with five male hotel employees standing behind him.

In a strong, deep voice, the police officer said, "Are you Tyson Hartnett?"

"Yes."

"Can I come in?"

"Sure."

The officer walked into the room. "So you want to kill yourself, huh?"

Taken aback by the direct question but not really having any defense for it, I just replied, "Yea I did before, but now I'm okay."

"I'm sure you are. So how were you thinking of doing it? Throwing yourself in front of a train? Jumping off a building?"

Wondering why he was asking me, I replied, "Probably the train…it'd be quicker."

He rifled through my backpack and pulled out a book. It was the Bible everybody on the team got about a year ago and that I read once in a while.

He flipped through it. "I guess *this* isn't helping."

I sheepishly responded, "I guess not."

He put down the Bible and checked out the rest of the room. Once he got done, he walked over and looked me directly in the eyes.

"Ok Mr. Tyson, we're taking you to the hospital now. You're spending the night there since you're a hazard to yourself."

I thought that was overboard and said, "No, I'm okay now. Really…I'm fine."

"That's great, but you're still coming with us."

Staring at the other staff members, I realized they weren't giving me a choice in the matter. After a few seconds, I resigned.

They walked me down to the lobby where a gurney waited for me. I climbed on and they wheeled me out through the lobby to the ambulance waiting outside. The lady behind the front desk stared at me and I was glad the lobby wasn't full of people. Even if nobody knew who I was, it was still embarrassing. They wheeled me into the ambulance and I laid back for the ride.

At the hospital, they wheeled me into a room with all white, barren walls. There were no machines or anything in the room except for the bed I was on. A girl outside the room kept watch on me through the little window in the door, and she looked eerily similar to Jamie. I calculated the odds of being able to off myself in this room, but it was impossible. I put the thought out of my mind as I laid back onto the bed.

--

For a few hours I just laid there looking at the blank walls. I tried to sleep but couldn't. Eventually, a psychiatrist came in and talked with me. He asked me easy questions to start, then more specific questions. Once I realized he wasn't there to judge me, I opened up and told him everything. He was the first person I told about what happened on the beach, and it felt cathartic to just get it off my chest.

He wrote down a few things and left the room. A few minutes later, I heard a guy moaning in the room next to me. I deciphered him saying, "The great thing is that if I die, she doesn't get any of my money! Hahaha!"

A few hours later a doctor came in and escorted me out to the waiting area, where my dad was standing. I said hi and gave him a hug. The psychiatrist who I spoke to earlier came over and explained to us that I was suffering from extreme depression. In his words, I had lost my identity because I was completely wrapped up in being "Tyson the basketball player." When basketball ended, I had no idea who I was anymore, and that's why I felt so lost. He said it would take time to re-establish who "Tyson" really was, possibly years. Hearing this, it was the first time I had heard anything like it. It made a lot of sense.

He said I could take pills if I wanted, but the important thing was to be around family. Getting a therapist would be a good idea so I could keep them updated on my progress. To me, this sounded a lot better than the other therapist I went to, who just told me to take a bunch of pills and I'd be okay. The psychiatrist gave us some paperwork and told me I was free to go.

Walking out of the hospital with my dad, I was grateful that he came up there in the middle of the night. I felt bad he had to pay for an expensive hotel, but I guess it was worth the investment. We went to the station and got the next train back to New York.

On the ride back, we didn't talk much. There were a few comments here and there, but nothing serious. He wasn't mad, something which I would have picked up on. It was just a dad being there for his son in a difficult time.

Looking back, he definitely saved my life.

--

At my dad's apartment in New York, we agreed that the best course of action was to go back to Jersey to spend some time with my mom and grandma. I stayed at my grandma's place for a few days, having deep discussions with her about what was going on. She didn't look at me as a freak, just as her grandson who needed extra love and attention at the moment.

When discussing my future, I planned to join Rutgers University for the spring semester and take classes as a regular student. I was still sick of basketball so that wasn't even in the cards. Craig was attending school at Rutgers, so I thought it'd be a perfect place to get back on my feet. The following weekend I went to the new student orientation to check out the campus.

At the orientation, it was extremely confusing trying to figure out which classes to take. When I was on the basketball team at Maine, the advisor made sure we took all the right courses. Our only job was to pass them. Here, there was a long line just to see if our calculus course from high school transferred over. It felt weird, plus the fact that everything was so spaced out made it even more confusing. I thought about how much easier this would be if I just played basketball.

On a Friday night, I tried to apply for Rutgers online. I filled out all the required fields on their website but when I put in the credit card, it said the payment didn't go through. The system was offline for maintenance from 10:50 PM to 11:00 PM every Friday night. I looked at the clock and it was 10:53 PM.

I just laughed at the chances of this. Considering how I wasn't too excited about going to Rutgers as only a student anyway, I logged out of the browser and shut the computer down. I wasn't going to pay the fee and I wasn't going to attend Rutgers. I didn't know what was next, but I'd figure it out.

--

When I told my mom about Rutgers, she agreed with my decision.

She asked, "If not Rutgers, then what?"

"Well since Rutgers was only going to accept half of my credits from Maine anyway, I would have basically wasted a year of college. I was thinking about going back to Maine, but only for school."

"Okay, but how will you pay for that if you're not on scholarship?"

"I'll get student loans and try to get financial aid."

"Okay, but what about Jamie? You're not doing this for her, are you?"

"No, I know that's over. Trust me. There are still lingering feelings but I'm not in that desperate mindset."

She laughed, "And what about the guys on the team? Will you be okay with seeing them again, even though you're not playing?"

I took a deep breath, "Yea, that will be weird, but I'll be okay with it. They'll understand. Lots of players quit basketball so I'll be just another one. Plus, I'll be able to meet new people since I won't have to be training all day long."

"Yea, that's a good point. Well I support you if that's what you want to do."

"I think that's the best thing, so I can start cultivating 'Tyson the person' as the psychiatrist said. I'll have some freedom and independence, and not only be dictated by a training schedule and what the coaches want from me."

I called the admittance office at Maine and it took only a few days to get everything squared away since I was already in the system. They told me classes started the next week, so I packed up what little I had. When I told my dad I was going back up to Maine for school, he told me he could help me move in as long as it was on the weekend. On a Friday night we took the eight-hour drive up to Orono in his car.

We took turns driving, and when we got there I told my dad I needed help with two things: A car and an apartment. Everything else I could handle myself. All day Saturday, I checked the Maine website for apartments. I got in touch with a guy who rented out rooms. It was a small place, with steps leading up to it right next to some train tracks. It had two small rooms, including a kitchen/living room. Since it was Orono, Maine, the price wasn't too expensive and I told him I liked it.

Next, my dad and I went to a car dealership. I found the cheapest car on the lot, a Nissan Versa, and we signed for it. At the end, my dad told me in a matter-of-fact way, "This is the last car I'm ever helping you out with."

Snow began falling pretty heavily as I drove it off the lot.

I stayed at the apartment that night while my dad stayed at a hotel. It was eerie being all alone, but it also felt liberating finally having my own place again. The next morning, my dad and I went shopping for furnishings. After that, I watched his car pull away as he headed for the lights of New York City, while I was once again living in Orono, Maine.

--

Having my own apartment felt amazing.

I didn't have to go to practice, I had the freedom to do what I wanted and I didn't have to listen to anybody. Going to classes, I felt like a normal human, not someone whose life was dictated through all hours of the day. I watched TV, attended after-school events and watched movies during the week. I even joined a rugby club since it seemed fun. After class I'd drive around with no particular destination, just enjoying my freedom.

I knew Jamie was in town but wanted nothing to do with her. I reached out to some people I knew from when I was playing basketball, and they didn't care if I played or not, they were just happy to see me again.

During a class, the professor asked the entire lecture hall if anybody played a sport on the team. He said, "If so, stand up."

I looked over at my friend and we just smiled. About fifteen athletes stood up and announced themselves, but the whole charade was over in less than a minute. They sat down again and the class resumed. I felt a twinge of regret, but also knew I had to stay strong with "Tyson the person."

Living the simple life for a few weeks was freeing, but it eventually got old. I began to do the same things over and over, and there was no more excitement. The loneliness at times became overwhelming, so I decided getting a therapist might help.

I searched around and found one nearby. On my first meeting with her, I told her about most things, but not everything. Her diagnosis was that I was co-dependent, and it made a lot of sense. Similar to what the psychiatrist in Boston said, she told me that my entire identity was wrapped up in playing basketball, then once that ended, I transferred that to Jamie. I had no balance in my life. For me, it was either all or nothing.

She referred me to a group called Co-Dependent's Anonymous, which was similar to Alcoholics Anonymous, but for people suffering with Co-Dependency. I told her I'd give it a try and she gave me the address. Arriving at the basement of a church on a cold, dark night, it was the first time I had ever experienced something like that. I saw similar meetings in movies and in one of Eminem's songs, but I never had any problems with alcohol since I was so focused on basketball.

Five people sat around a table as the leader stated the rules for the program. Like in AA, one person spoke their name, with everybody responding, "Hi

_____." Then, the person started talking about their situation. Nobody talked or judged, just listened. When it was my turn to speak, I was hesitant to open up. However, listening to everybody else's story gave me the confidence to say what I wanted.

When it was my turn to speak, I said, "Hi, thanks for letting me attend. My name is Tyson."

In unison, everybody replied, "Hi Tyson."

I didn't tell them everything, just said what was on my mind. When I finished, it felt like God just lifted my whole chest up to the sky. At that moment I understood why these groups were so powerful. When everybody finished, I read the twelve steps, donated a few dollars, and drove back to the apartment.

I kept attending the meetings and seeing the therapist. She suggested I do more exercising since I wasn't doing much physical activity. I didn't want to go to the gym on campus though, because I didn't want people to see me and ask why I wasn't playing basketball, or even worse, run into Jamie. Instead, I forced myself to do pushups and run around the neighborhood as much as possible. When I started doing these things, it refreshed my mind and made me feel amazing.

One night, I called Phil to see how he was doing. He told me to come to a teammate's apartment so we could hang out. At first I was hesitant, but then I realized these were still my friends and they probably wouldn't make fun of me for not playing basketball. I drove over there and they were playing video games.

They asked what I was doing back in Maine, and I explained it was my best option since all my credits went through. They asked if I was still playing basketball and I told them I quit because I was sick of it.

When I said that, one of my teammates from the past year said, "I don't blame you, man. I wish I could quit."

I was surprised when he said that, but it also opened my eyes to the fact that I wasn't the only one who felt burnt out from basketball.

Still, after two months of living the simple life at the apartment, I needed a change. Things were just too boring. Going to school was easy, but then the rest of the day I had nothing else to do. None of the groups on campus excited me and I didn't feel like I was doing anything important.

The apartment was right next to a train track, and every night a train would rumble by, shaking the walls. When this happened, I questioned what the hell I was doing there. Yes, I had to finish school, but that was the easy part. I felt like I needed a challenge, and I wasn't going to get that challenge living the simple life in Orono.

--

Spring break started the following week, so my plan was to head down to New Jersey and figure out my future once I got there. I called my mom to tell her what I was thinking and she supported me once again. I put as many things as I could in the Versa but left the rest in a storage locker to pick up later. I hadn't made a payment yet for the semester at Maine, so I wouldn't be wasting any money.

On one of my final nights at the apartment before Spring break, I walked outside and heard music blasting from down the street. I walked over to take a look and noticed a huge house party. Since I had nothing else to do, I entered the house and joined the fun.

People immediately started offering me shots and I obliged. I didn't know anybody, but still joined in their screaming and dancing. I got pretty wasted. When I was ready to leave I went to the closet to pick up my jacket. Looking around, I couldn't find it. I searched for about five minutes but eventually realized somebody had stolen it.

My wallet was in there, but I fortunately left my keys in my pants pocket. I was worried about the driver's license though because I had a long drive ahead. Wondering what I was going to do, I staggered back to the apartment and fell asleep.

The following morning, I still didn't know what I was going to do. I went out to the car to run some errands, and as I unlocked the door I saw my driver's license lying there face up in the snow with my pretty face staring back at me.

I laughed and looked up at the sky. "God, you're just messing with me, right?"

He said, "No, Tyson. I'm not messing with you. Get your shit together."

Relieved, I listened to Him and prepared for my trip back to Jersey. I had some cash in the apartment, so I used that for gas and tolls along the way. On the final night in Orono, I stayed up all night listening to a country music station on the radio. It felt peaceful, being in the boonies of Maine and listening to singers moan about their lives. However, I knew I had to get out.

The next day, I packed up the Versa and drove south once again.

5
A RE-BIRTH

It was warming up in Medford as spring approached. I lifted weights outside and soaked up the sun's rays. Gil and Jamie were still on my mind but I knew I couldn't let them overwhelm me. I trusted that God had a plan for me, and I was going to fulfill it. Being a regular student at Maine for a while, I realized that life wasn't for me. It was too boring and it seemed like all anybody did was party and drink.

Outside one day, I picked up a basketball and started dribbling. I was immediately transported back to my freshman year of high school, shooting in the cold, trying to get as many minutes as I could on the JV team. I thought about how life took some weird turns, but at that moment the smell and feeling of the ball in my hands felt so good.

I kept dribbling, eventually walking out to the street in front of the house. For over an hour, I did the same dribbling drills I performed years earlier, mixing in different moves like there was someone playing defense on me. My handle was horrible, but after every dribble I felt myself getting it back ever so slightly. When I finished dribbling, I shot for a few minutes in the driveway. It felt amazing, and I wondered why I had given this up in the first place.

Following the psychiatrist's advice, I tried to exercise as much as possible. It gave me a sense of power after every session, also providing me with clarity of what I wanted to do in the future.

An interesting thing about my life was that when I played basketball, I'd typically eat very well that day. Even when I was nearly broke, it was like I gave myself permission to eat. When I didn't play, I was very frugal and worried about every dime I had. From this realization, I thought, *Things are good when I play basketball.*

An old friend who still lived in the area pushed me to play with him at some courts nearby. I told him I was rusty and out of shape, but he kept pushing me. Eventually I gave in and went with him. Being around the guys and playing again felt amazing. It was the same trash talking I grew up with, and I actually still had game. I wasn't scoring every play but the talent was there. I knew, and felt in my bones, that there was potential.

Back at the house, I contemplated what I wanted to do next. Basketball was sneaking its way back into my life, but I knew the dangers of overdoing it. I told myself to take it slow.

Day after day, week after week, the drive and urge to play consumed me more and more. When I went to the gym, I started to score even more points. If I knew a guy played in college somewhere, I went at him, trying to prove I was better. I focused on defense and rebounding, the high-level instruction from Maine propelling my actions.

One day after playing, I sat my mom down and told her, "I think I want to play basketball again."

We discussed it and I called Rick the next day. I hadn't talked to Rick in over a year because I was embarrassed about what happened at Maine. I felt that if I didn't play basketball, he didn't care about me.

Rick picked up, "What's up Scooby Doo?? Where are youuuuu?"

"What's up Rick?" I said, laughing. "I think I want to play basketball again."

"Oh yea? Well you're not going to be able to play D1."

"I know, I know. But I just want to play, now. I don't care where it is. I got the urge to play man, and I know I can play somewhere."

"Okay, well I'll start making some calls and asking around. Just get back into shape. You've been out of it for a while."

"You're right man, I'm doing that now."

Rick ended with his signature line, "Word. I wanna be like you when I grow up!"

In terms of my eligibility to play college basketball, I redshirted my first year at Maine but then went back for a semester, so I now had two and a half years remaining. I didn't care where I played at this point, I just wanted to play.

My mom was a huge help. She gave me a piece of paper with a line down the middle and told me to write what I wanted in a school on the left and what I didn't want on the right. Exhaust yourself and don't hold back, she said.

I had never done this exercise before, but even before I did it I knew it was going to be a huge help. The first thing I wanted was for basketball to not be so serious. I liked to play, but didn't want the intensity of a Division 1 program. Something challenging yet less structured would be perfect.

Second, I wanted to have a social life. I wanted to meet people, have friends, and establish relationships. I also preferred to be driving distance from the beach in New Jersey, although I wasn't sure why.

Finally, I wrote that I wanted to be "The Man" again. I was sick of getting pushed around and being a bum. I wanted to re-find the swag and confidence I hadn't experienced in a long time.

I kept the paper around and looked at it often because my mom said that if I consistently visualized what I wrote, it would soon become a reality. I had my doubts but figured I needed all the help I could get.

While looking for colleges, my mom also got me in touch with a landscaper who needed help with basic lawn care. Working for him, it felt good to perform some manual labor and make some money.

Eventually, I got in touch with a coach from a small Division 3 school in Delaware who wanted me on the team. He invited me to check it out and meet some of the current players. I drove down but there was nobody on campus and it seemed too small. The coach was a nice guy, but I decided this wasn't the place for me. It just didn't feel right.

In Medford, I called my dad and told him my plans to play basketball again. He supported the idea, as long as it was what I wanted. Since I had a plan for my life now, he said he'd be able to get me an internship in New York

City for the summer. I could stay at his place while I worked and got ready for the basketball season. The landscaping job was only part time, so I went up to New York one day to interview for the position. It seemed like a cool place in the heart of New York City, so I accepted the role.

That weekend in New York, I went into a church one morning since I needed answers on what I should do. I was hoping for a sign...a calling...anything.

There, I prayed, "God, help me with my path. I know I want to play basketball, but don't know where I should play. Please give me a sign or direction so I know what to do."

I sat there for a few minutes in silence. Nothing happened. A few more minutes and still nothing. I thought, *Well, whatever. I guess that didn't work.*

I stood up, said a parting prayer, then walked out of the church into the sunlight. Back on the street, I checked my phone. It said I had one missed call and a voicemail. I pressed the button and listened.

"Hey Tyson, this is Coach Cassidy from Rowan University. I know you're looking for a school to play at, and I'd love to have you down to the campus to check it out and play with the guys. Let me know if you're interested and if so, give me a call back."

I dropped the phone from my ear and almost started crying. Wow. When I was in church, my phone was on silent so Coach Cassidy was probably calling me right as I was praying. I asked for a sign and got one in a big way.

I called Coach Cassidy back and he told me when the guys would be playing the following week. Rowan is in Glassboro, New Jersey, which was only about 45 minutes from my house, so it was an easy drive. We set up a time for me to come down and he seemed genuinely excited. After what just happened, I was excited too. My body wasn't in basketball shape, but I knew I could get there in no time.

The following week I went to play with the guys and it felt amazing. The trash talking, camaraderie, and intensity was something I had missed. I didn't play that well, but after years of training with Division 1 athletes I knew I could get my game back quickly.

While playing, there was also a moment in which I knew I could be a great player at the school. I had the ball on offense at the three-point line as a teammate moved to set a screen on my defender. I took advantage of the opportunity, pulled up for the shot, and missed, but I saw that there was enough room for me to work my magic when I got my stamina and quickness back. After the intensity of Division 1, I saw things during the games I would have never seen before.

When we finished playing, the guys showed me the locker room and drove me around campus. They explained what it was like on the team and what to expect. Everyone was genuine and I felt the love. Some of the guys even knew me from playing at Shawnee when I was one of the best in the state. They had a lot of respect that I played at a Division 1 school for two years, even if I didn't actually play at all.

Driving the 45 minutes back to Medford, Rowan felt right. When I got back I looked at the sheet of what I wanted in a school. Going down the list, everything fit. Glassboro, NJ was close to Philadelphia, so close to a major city...check. An hour from the beach...check. Less stressful than Division 1...from what I had seen so far, check. Able to have a social life with great people...check. The potential to be "The Man" again...definite check. It amazed me that everything I wrote down was exactly what Rowan turned out to be.

Making the decision still wasn't easy. Years before, Rick had said that if I couldn't make it up at Maine, I could always play at Rowan. At the time, I didn't want to even think about that since I thought of myself as a Division 1 player, and anything other than that was beneath me. However, at this point in my life, Rowan was looking like a great option. I decided I needed to move beyond the more simplistic mindset I had had in the past. I just wanted to play again. So after a few more days of thought, I made my decision.

Rowan was where I'd finish up my basketball career. They couldn't give me a full scholarship, but since I was in state, tuition was a lot cheaper. Coach Cassidy also said I'd be able to get financial aid, something I'd have to work out with the administrative office.

--

For the summer, I slept on my dad's couch in New York while I worked at the internship. It wasn't perfect but I had structure and a future. I worked Tuesday, Wednesday and Thursday and put in a lot of time training for the upcoming season. When people asked about me, they got excited that I played basketball, but I tried not to get labeled as "Tyson the basketball player." I wanted to be "Tyson the person," who would soon be playing basketball in college. Nothing more.

To stay in shape, I joined a basketball league in New York City. The team was mediocre but it was the perfect ground to get my game back. In one of the first games as we lined up for a free throw, all the years of basketball came rushing back to me. The sweat, the smell of the gym, and the respect of the battle between the players made me feel good to be back. I thought, *Tyson, why would you ever leave this?*

Then a moment occurred during the NBA Draft in 2008 that really made me look at my life. I heard that a teammate from my sixth grade team, Jason Thompson, was slated to get drafted. In his high school years, he grew to 6'10" tall and then played four years at Rider University, where he was the top scorer and rebounder nearly every season. I followed the draft online. When the twelfth pick arrived I saw that it was Jason. He was now an instant millionaire.

I thought about how different our lives were at that moment. Here I was, working this little internship and sleeping on my dad's couch, barely having enough money for a Metrocard to get to work, while Jason was now a multi-millionaire in the NBA.

I knew he was a better player, taller, and stronger, but I still felt regrets. I thought about if I could have worked harder or done more. Being 6'10" helped, but other guys who were drafted were 6'6", as tall as me. I felt like a bum, but tried to not let the feelings of guilt and regret overwhelm me.

--

I had high hopes for my new life at Rowan, with basketball a part of it but not an overwhelming force.

On move-in day, I drove the Versa to Glassboro, New Jersey. When I got there I had no idea where to go, so I asked an older guy who was volunteering. He pointed me in the right direction and, for me, this was a huge moment.

Anything I do in life, I analyze the first moments of the journey. I planned on being there for two years so I was looking for signs of what was to come. If this older guy was rude and indifferent, I'd see it as a sign that the rest of my experience would be similar. Fortunately, he was pleasant.

I brought my bags to the dorm, where I was assigned a small room. Coach Cassidy had helped me get a single room so I could stay focused. Once I settled in, I went to the gym to meet the new players.

Most of them I didn't know, but they knew of me as "the Division 1 transfer." I was okay with that since it gave me credibility. Being taller and stronger than most of them, it was evident I had spent time on a vigorous training schedule. They looked up to me and I was glad all the hard work wasn't in vain.

We didn't scrimmage that day, but the next day we got together and played. Since it was Division 3, no coaches showed up at our dorms reminding us of the mandatory practice. If guys had other obligations, they were free to take care of them. It was important to show up to workouts, but the coaches wouldn't kick anybody off the team if they didn't show.

After a week of getting back into the swing of things, I knew I would destroy this Division 3 competition. I still had my shot and court vision, even though my quickness needed work. I knew once I played consistently I'd get it all back. The other guys were solid players, but banging against Division 1 bodies at Maine for two years gave me a huge advantage. I learned so many subtle things about the game that someone wouldn't know unless they'd been through it.

Everybody on the team was cool and they introduced me to tons of new people. My goal was to develop friendships away from basketball, and that's exactly what was happening. Since I was the new guy, a few times people tried to fight or test me. I didn't back down, but I wasn't going to get in trouble by fighting someone unless it really came down to it. The fact that the guys on the team had my back made me feel even better about choosing Rowan.

Now that I didn't have to train for four hours every day anymore, I gave myself liberty to do what I wanted. I hooked up a PlayStation 3 and played online games for hours on the weekends or at night. I hung out with guys across the hall or watched mindless TV after workouts. I asked girls out on dates, and if they rejected me I didn't worry about it. I just moved onto the next one and got to know somebody else.

It felt healthy, like this was what normal people did. I made sure to stay disciplined but also loved the freedom.

--

When practices officially started on October 15th, I was ready. However, before every practice I still got scared. All the fear and worry I felt at Maine rushed back to me as if I were one of Pavlov's dogs.

Still, I turned out to be the best player. I proved it in the preseason scrimmages, but I still got scared that I was going to mess up and never play on the team. To me, basketball practice was associated with: If you mess up, you will never play at this school.

Rowan practices were hard, but they weren't impossible. We did lots of running to build our stamina while getting a feel for who had what skill sets. After practices, we all hung out in the locker room, talked trash and ragged on each other. Who had the hottest sister was a constant debate. Nobody was left out and it seemed like everybody was friends with each other. I even spoke up sometimes instead of sitting quietly in the corner. It was real, genuine camaraderie with guys who loved to play basketball.

On the school side, it was difficult to get back into the swing of things, but I worked at it. I was majoring in Business Management and my grades suffered for the first few months, but I made sure to get them back up. It was all about what the teachers were looking for on tests and homework.

Finally, official games began and I was named a starter. Coach Cassidy, true to his word, played me about thirty minutes every game. It was amazing being back on the court, in the tip-off circle to start the game, and then having the freedom to play my game when I got in. It was exactly what I hoped for when I transferred to this Division 3 school.

Every game, I earned my starting spot. One game I'd have 20 points, the next I'd have 12 rebounds, the next I'd have 20 points *and* 12 rebounds. I proved that I was a solid player and teams treated me as an offensive threat. We won games, too, which was the important part.

One of my best games of the year came during a holiday tournament. It was the championship of a four-team series on our home floor. At the time, it didn't feel like I was shooting a lot, just taking shots that were in the flow of the game. I didn't think I made that many, either.

However, after we won the championship, the announcer said, "And the MVP of the tournament... with 37 points in the championship game... Tyson Hartnett!"

I looked at my other teammates with a shocked expression and said, "What?!"

37 points?! To me, and to my teammates, that was ridiculous. I wondered how and when I made so many shots. It was the highest point total I had since I scored 36 back at Shawnee. In the locker room, all my teammates congratulated me. It was an amazing moment and I soaked it all in.

--

As the season progressed, we held a record just above .500. I continued to play thirty minutes per game and do what I could for the team. It was exactly what I hoped for, and exactly what I needed.

Off the court, I continued to live an authentic college life. I went on dates with girls, hung out with friends, and went with the flow of the social sphere. Occasionally the school newspaper featured me, which provided even more publicity around campus. Meeting different types of people, it was refreshing to discuss different topics, not just the same locker room talk I'd hear every day.

With all this newfound attention, I never hinted to anybody what I had been through over the past two years. If anybody asked, I simply replied, "I took a year off." One of the assistant coaches, Dave Lafferty, told me halfway through the season that he had seen me when I was working at Burlington Coat Factory. He didn't say anything, but had probably thought I was just another high school athlete who turned into a bum. For a while, he was right.

With our record, we barely sneaked into the playoffs. We won the first game but then lost in the second round. Once the season was over, I didn't mind, since I had another year left. The first year was just about getting accustomed to basketball once again and meeting as many people as I could.

I finished the season as the leading scorer and rebounder on the team. I averaged about 15 points per game with about 6 rebounds. I made the All-Conference team and had received the Player of the Week Award a few times during the season. I was back, and it felt so good.

The year ended with a Spring Fest at one of the apartment complexes nearby. Thousands of students from Rowan were outside, having fun and enjoying the day. I soaked in the moment, knowing it was light years away from where I was only a year ago.

At one point in my life, I had seen a TV show about a prehistoric animal. The story was fiction, but after my first year at Rowan I realized I had a lot in common with that animal.

Here's a synopsis of the story:

This animal was one of the smallest on its island, fighting to survive every single day. There were dozens of predators all around him and he had to watch his back constantly. One day, a huge storm flooded the island, killing almost everything.

The storm washed the animal out to sea, then to another island. He was so weak he couldn't even open his eyes, living in a state of near-death for days. Other animals from the new island came up to him, wondering what he was and where he came from. After about a week, this animal opened his eyes for the first time, looking at his surroundings with curiosity. He was frail, but his heart and legs still worked. Standing up, he looked around, no idea where he was.

Slowly, he regained his strength and started walking around the island. To his surprise, there were no predators, with nothing chasing him. In fact, he was the biggest animal on the island. When he stopped to eat, he didn't have to worry about his life. When the other animals saw him, they looked up to him in awe, wondering where he came from. He was bigger and stronger than all the other living creatures, but didn't prey on them since he ate plants.

This animal remembered everything he experienced on his previous island and was grateful that he survived. He now had free reign to live how he wanted on this island, with all the other creatures looking up to him.

--

When the school year wrapped up, my guidance counselor told me I needed to take summer classes if I wanted to graduate on time. I didn't have any other plans for the summer, so I agreed. A friend who I met during the school year named Mike was also going to be taking classes. He had an apartment off campus and told me I could stay with him if I paid rent.

While the school year at Rowan was fun and energetic, the summer was barren. Most of the students went home and there was nothing more to do than work out, go to class, then play video games. Class was only a few hours per day, so I needed something else to do in the meantime. A few other athletes who were around worked a job doing maintenance between their classes, so I joined them.

Nights and weekends got extremely boring though, so I wanted to use that time to be productive, not just see if I could get to the World Series in MLB 2008 on my PlayStation 3. In New York one weekend, my dad's friend suggested the idea of being a bouncer. I thought about it and it seemed like an interesting job. I thought I could work at a nightclub, talking with hot girls and breaking up fights.

I scouted out venues in Philadelphia and started applying. Sending out a few dozen resumes, I hoped I'd hear back quickly. However, almost nobody was hiring, except for one place right off Chestnut Street in Center City.

When I went for the interview, the outside looked like a big warehouse and I wondered if I was in the right place. Behind the counter was an Asian guy with tattoos.

He looked me over and said, "Hey, we're closed."

"Oh, I'm applying to be a bouncer. Theresa told me to come by at this time."

He looked me up and down again. "I see. Are you gay enough to work here?"

Thinking that was a weird question, I just replied, "Um, yea I guess."

"Ok, well she'll be right out. Fill out this application."

I filled out the form and waited. After a few minutes Theresa arrived and we walked over to the desolate bar off the side of the massive dance floor. She asked me a bunch of questions and I told her I was willing to work nights and weekends, basically whenever they needed me. I found out the place was open every night from 7 PM to 4 AM, so it'd be a perfect job to keep me occupied. She hired me on the spot, telling me when I needed to show up for my first shift.

On my first night working, everything came into perspective. Looking around, I was wondering why there weren't many girls and why some of the guys were getting a little close to each other. That's when it hit me... it was a gay club.

All throughout the summer, I never had to break up one fight. Some of the guys got too drunk or went into the bathroom together, but that was the extent of it. Girls came up to me sometimes, frustrated that no guys were hitting on them. They'd ask me, "Are you straight?"

When I told them yes, their eyes lit up and we'd start to talk. The whole experience was interesting.

I worked at the gay bar at night and a maintenance job on campus during the day. In between, I played video games and worked out as much as I could.

Summer eventually came to a close as Coach Cassidy told me of a transfer coming in named Pete who needed a roommate. When we met, we immediately got along, so we decided to room together in an apartment right near where I stayed that summer. The area was known for its parties, so I knew it was going to be a fun senior year.

--

Throughout my life, I'd never been a partier. I was always focused, determined, and disciplined in how I could achieve the next level of success in my basketball career. This year though, I wanted to have fun and be "The Man."

When school started again, we got a few new faces on the team. Everything was similar to the year before, except for the fact I was living in the new apartment with Pete. The new guys looked up to me, since they knew I was the leading scorer and rebounder from the previous season.

During the week we trained and on the weekend we partied. Pete had a huge group of friends, so he brought them over on weekends and we'd all drink and blast music. On one of the first weekends, we had a house warming party where we bumped Jay-Z's *Blueprint 3* until the sun came up. We invited our new teammates over because I wanted to make them feel included, not as outcasts just because they were new. I knew what that feeling was like and it sucked.

This was my last year of college, so I didn't feel too guilty about drinking and partying as much as I could. During the week, I made sure to do my homework and workouts, but on the weekend we'd fill as many people as we could into the apartment and just rage. Sometimes I'd go from party to party until I eventually passed out in my bed or somewhere else. Up until that point in my life I'd never blacked out, but it happened more than once that semester. It was weird not remembering anything that happened, only having it replayed to me by my friends at breakfast the next day.

To flush the toxins from my system, I ran about five miles every Monday morning. I didn't have class on Monday so I needed that to keep structure in my life. I lifted weights afterwards but didn't shoot as much. I felt I'd have my shot regardless, but knew being in shape was the most important thing for the season.

When the games started in my senior year of college, I proved once again that I was the best on the team. I averaged about 20 points per game, adding in about 8 rebounds over the first few contests. I even got featured in the school newspaper again, along with a photo of me during a game. Lots of other students saw it and were impressed.

After the games, we didn't have the discipline like we had at Division 1. Instead of eating, hydrating and resting, most of us just went back to the apartment and started drinking. A moment when we played a beer-drinking game after a win was when I really noticed the difference. I sarcastically said to them, "Ok guys, now we should be hydrating and getting protein to make up for the lost nutrients during the game."

They all started laughing and somebody said, "Beer has nutrients man, and it's hydrating me pretty well right now."

As a team we racked up the wins and headed into the Christmas break with a 10-2 record. For my stats, I averaged about 20 points with 10 rebounds per game, receiving the Player of the Week Award once or twice. I even received the MVP of the holiday tournament again, averaging 20 points per game.

When I went out to Chicago for Christmas, some of my family members asked me what I was going to do when I graduated. I admitted I didn't know yet, but said I had time to figure it out. In reality, I had absolutely no idea. My only focus was the basketball season and enjoying the ride along the way. I figured once I finished I'd get a job somewhere, but didn't know exactly where that would be.

Rick had brought up the idea at one point about possibly playing professional basketball overseas, but I knew those teams wouldn't want a low-level Division 3 player. They wanted high-level Division 1 guys who could jump through the roof. To me, the idea was a pipe dream so I wasn't going to worry about it.

--

Getting back from Christmas break, we played an important game against Stockton, one of our biggest rivals. During the match, I went up to block a shot on a player but as my hand came down, it landed hard on his nose. His nose and my knuckle started bleeding, so we went over to the trainers to get it patched up. We both played the rest of the game without any problems.

When I woke up the next day, my entire knuckle hurt. At first, I thought it was just the wound healing, but after a few hours it started to swell up. By the end of the day, it looked like one of those inflatable balloon hands. It hurt to even move, so I went to the trainer to see what the heck was happening. After inspection, they told me the wound most likely got infected, so they gave me antibiotics to handle it.

For days, my hand hurt to move. If it was below my heart, all the blood rushed to it. The pain sometimes kept me up at night and I couldn't even dribble a basketball.

It wasn't the worst injury that could happen, but it ruined the flow of the season. While I was in shape and focused before the injury, I now had to stay out of practices for over a week trying to get my hand back to normal. On weekends I'd still party, using my good hand to drink beer.

After two weeks the swelling in my hand went back to normal, but I was out of sync. Not being in practice for two weeks made me a step slower, and it took a few games to get used to playing again. Coach Cassidy eased me into my return, only playing me sparingly while he monitored my progress. This hurt my average points per game, which had been at 20 but began to get lower and lower. I thought, *If I had any shot at playing overseas, no way would a team want me now. Nobody's going to sign a player only averaging 15 points per game at a Division 3 school.*

When I finally got better, only a few games remained in the season. Our record suffered with the tough conference schedule, and we barely snuck into the playoffs. In the first round, we played a tall, athletic team from Ramapo. We were neck and neck with them all game, but they won by one point from a tip-in at the buzzer.

Just like that, the season, and my college basketball career, were finished.

I cared that we lost but not as much as I should have. The alcohol I had been drinking over the past few months really started to catch up. I was lethargic, didn't have much motivation, and nothing really excited me except for parties.

One day at practice before the season ended, Coach Cassidy asked, "Tyson, are you hung over? You aren't even jumping for rebounds."

I replied, "Nah, Coach I'm okay. I don't drink much."

With a skeptical look, he said, "Tyson, I can smell the alcohol coming off you right now."

When the season finished, practices finished as well. My daily structure was gone and I'd sometimes watch ESPN for hours. I still had no idea what to do when school finished, but knew eventually I'd figure it out.

As for the apartment, it was a mess. Months of parties and alcohol almost completely destroyed it. Big chunks of the wall were taken out, the carpet was saturated with beer, and the kitchen was extremely sticky and falling apart. I tried to fix the wall, clean the carpet and restore the kitchen, but it was no use. A professional had to fix them all and it got tacked onto the bill once we left the room.

I didn't take care of myself and I started getting lazy. The registration on the Nissan Versa had expired, but I procrastinated in renewing it. One day when I was going to the liquor store, I saw that it was closed, so I did a U-Turn in the middle of the street. At the end of the street was a cop, who proceeded to pull me over. I pulled into a shopping center and noticed a family with young kids staring at me. They probably thought I was a criminal.

When the officer found out my registration was expired, he said, "You know, I could impound your car because of this, but it's your first offense so I'm not going to. Just get your tags renewed."

I thanked him, realizing it was a close call. But a few weeks later, I had another problem with the Versa that turned out to be much worse.

One night driving home from campus with some friends, we stopped at a red light. In front of us was an SUV. They saw a bus take the turn a little too tight so they backed up. Backing up too far, they plowed straight into the front of the Versa. When the light turned green they pulled into a parking lot nearby. I followed them and we all got out to inspect the damage.

Normally in this situation, someone calls the police, a report is created, insurance cards are swapped, and every detail is noted. I wasn't drunk at the time, but everything I did then was lazy. This was no exception.

When the kid saw the damage, he said, "No problem, I'll pay for it, but I really need to get to baseball practice." The damage wasn't severe, but the hood of the car was bent in. I related with being late for practice so we exchanged information, trusting that we'd be in touch within the next few days.

When I called him the next day, he didn't pick up. Same thing the day after. After a few days, I called the insurance company to tell them what happened. Since I only had a phone number, the insurance representative told me she'd give the number a try. When she called back, I got bad news. She said he denied everything and hung up. I was mad at myself for thinking I could trust this kid.

There was slight damage to the hood and I procrastinated in getting that fixed, too. Driving down the highway one night, the entire hood flipped up onto the windshield. I couldn't see anything so I pulled over. Evidently the latch that kept the hood down had broken. I drove the rest of the way home at 25 miles per hour so the hood didn't fly up again. When I got back to the apartment, I secured the hood with a plastic tie because I couldn't afford to take it to the shop.

As school winded down, I still had no idea what I wanted to do next. I asked Coach Cassidy if he knew of anywhere I could work, but he didn't know anyone hiring at the moment. I was extremely lazy and was not taking care of myself or my future.

--

One of the final parties of the year was Spring Fest, the same one as the previous year and held in the courtyard right outside our apartment. It was a great day and lots of fun. When the afternoon came around, some police officers started to show up. They wanted to end the party, so they began handing out tickets to anyone with a red cup. Even if there was nothing in the cup, they'd still give that person a ticket.

Standing outside my apartment, I watched from a distance as the cops made a show of force. I had a cup in my hand but figured if they started to come towards me I'd go back inside or drop it. Just then, an officer sneaked around the corner and shouted, "Hey you, come over here!"

I didn't know if he was shouting at me but I didn't want to find out. I turned around, walked into the apartment and closed the door. After a few seconds, there was a knock on the door. I didn't answer until there was another knock. I put down the cup and walked outside.

The young officer said, "I saw you with that cup. You're not allowed to have that out here."

"Okay, I know, I'm sorry about that. It's gone."

He shot back, "Where is your ID?"

I didn't want another ticket because I was already dealing with the car situation, so I replied, "I don't have it."

"You don't have your ID in your apartment?"

"No, I don't."

"Okay smart guy, what's your name?"

At this point, a few other officers came up behind him for backup. Across the courtyard, I saw Mike and a few other friends watching the whole thing.

Not wanting to get in trouble, I made up a name, and the officer behind him said, "Okay, we're going to see if there is anybody at Rowan with that name."

He called into the Rowan system, but they said nobody with that name went to Rowan.

When the younger officer heard that, he freaked out. "You're giving us false information, and for that you're getting arrested!"

I said, "What?! For what?!"

He grabbed the handcuffs from his back pocket and told me to turn around.

I said, "What are you doing?? I didn't do anything!"

He grabbed me, starting to turn me around so he could cuff me. He screamed, "Stop resisting arrest! You're resisting!!"

I had no idea what was happening, but I knew that resisting arrest was a big deal. I didn't want any more problems so I just let him cuff me. He turned me around and walked me out to the courtyard.

As I was led across the big stretch of open courtyard, everybody started to take notice. When they all recognized it was me, they started cheering and chanting my name, "TY-SON...TY-SON...TY-SON!!!"

I overheard one of the officers behind me say, "Well, I guess we know his real name now."

The young officer put me into the car and drove me to the campus police station. They handcuffed me to a pole while I took a seat. An older officer behind a computer looked over at me and said in a stern manner, "What are you here for?"

I replied, "For holding a cup and giving a fake name."

His expression immediately changed to a look that said, "Are you kidding me? They arrested you for that?"

I answered his questions and sat there for an hour. Finally, he gave me a ticket and told me a court appearance was mandatory. He unlocked the handcuffs and told me I was free to go. The police station wasn't far from campus, so I walked the twenty minutes back to the apartment. When I told everyone what had happened, they just laughed.

Freaking red solo cup.

--

One thing I noticed about all these minor problems was that I wasn't moving forward. I still had no idea what I wanted to do after college, didn't have any jobs lined up and wasn't working to push or develop myself. As I dealt with one problem, another one popped up. In hindsight, I would have done things a lot differently.

After the arrest, the judge required me to perform forty hours of community service. Every Saturday morning at 8:00 AM, I put on a bright orange vest and picked up trash in Glassboro. I knew I wasn't a felon, so I treated it as a way to see society from a different perspective.

School finished and I needed to take one more class to graduate in the summer. It wasn't a difficult class but I still had to show up. There was nobody on campus, so I drove up to New York one weekend with a friend to experience the city. On Sunday, I started the hour-long drive back down to South Jersey with him, his girlfriend, and another friend.

I was driving down the New Jersey turnpike right outside the city. It was a tight stretch of the highway, with only a small shoulder on the side. We were all having a pleasant time and I felt happy school was going to be over with soon.

Just then, the hood flew up onto the windshield again. This time, it shattered the glass. I ducked low so I could see where I was driving and pumped the brakes, pulling over to the tight shoulder.

Everyone in the car was freaking out as I got out and took a look. It didn't completely shatter the glass, but there were large spider cracks everywhere. I discovered that the plastic ties had ripped right off.

This was bad news because I definitely couldn't drive all the way back to school like this. If the hood flipped up again, the windshield could completely shatter. I went into the backseat and found my final two twist-ties to secure the hood again.

My friend's girlfriend lived nearby and she said I could park the Versa outside her house for the time being. I had to attend class at Rowan the next day, so I needed to get back down there that night. With everyone else in the backseat, I slowly drove the ten minutes to the girl's house, praying the hood wouldn't fly up in the meantime. I got us back there safely and parked along the street. She said it would be fine for a week or two, but I couldn't leave it there much longer than that.

Before we left, I put a piece of paper on the windshield with my name and contact information in case someone were to tow it. We got in the girl's car as I took a final look at the Versa, the car I had been through so much with.

It seemed so sad, cracked, and broken on the side of the road. I made a promise to myself I'd get it fixed as soon as possible.

About a week later, I got a call from the Secaucus police department. They told me my car had been towed and labeled as an abandoned vehicle. The officer suggested I come get it as soon as possible, otherwise there would be daily holding fees.

I took a bus to New York to meet my aunt and uncle, and they took me to get the car. I got a ticket for an abandoned vehicle and my uncle loaned me $350 to get the car from the impound lot. Getting the windshield fixed was also expensive, but it needed to get done. Once the Versa was back to normal, I was mad at myself for letting it all happen.

Looking back, all the training and work I put in was destroyed from the alcohol. I could have possibly scored more points or won more games, but the alcohol consumed my life. All the hours of sweat and training I put in during the week were destroyed on the weekends. The worst part is that the younger guys looked up to me. They saw me as the leading scorer and best player, yet I didn't have a work ethic. All I did was drink and party. I was a terrible role model for the new guys. If I had another chance, I would have resisted the temptation of alcohol and partying, focusing instead on developing my body and looking forward to life after college.

I still didn't know what I wanted to do but New York seemed like a good place to start so I applied for jobs online. I heard back from a few companies with sales positions but nothing worked out. Two weeks after I got my car back, I finished my summer class and was officially a college graduate.

Around that time I received a message on Facebook asking if I was interested in playing in a South Jersey Legends All-Star Game. Looking at the roster, I saw many of the guys I played with growing up, including some who were playing professionally. When I saw Jason Thompson's name on the list, I immediately agreed.

The season had been over for a few months so I wasn't in the best basketball shape, but it was an All-Star Game. Nobody ever played real defense in these games; it was about fancy shots and high-flying dunks to entertain the crowd. I wasn't a high-flyer so my goal was to make a few shots, play solid defense and reunite with the guys I grew up with.

The game was at Glassboro High School, right next to Rowan, and it felt like a basketball reunion. Some guys were playing overseas, some were finishing college and Jason was doing well in the NBA. Seeing him in person, it was evident he had been playing against the biggest guys on the planet for the past few years.

In warmups, these guys put on a show. Many of them had forty-inch vertical leaps and it was impressive, even to me. When the game started I was put in as a substitute, which was fine with me. Most of these guys had played high Division 1 for four years, so just being on the court with them gave me a sense of pride.

When I finally got in, I played my role. I took smart shots, passed when necessary, and tried to defend Jason as best I could. He was tall and had more power than I had even expected.

During one play, I went for a loose ball at half court against Jason's younger brother Ryan. Both of our hands hit the ball but he slapped it away. The next play on offense, I got the ball in the corner and lined up for the shot. When my right pinky finger touched the ball, it felt like the ball was flat. I took the shot and missed.

I then looked down at my finger. It jutted way out to the right, and I couldn't feel anything. I was praying it was only jammed. When halftime came, I showed it to the trainers.

One of them said, "Oh yea, that thing's broken. You should go to the hospital."

Taking her advice, I called my roommate Pete to take me to the hospital since I didn't have GPS on my phone. X-rays verified that it was indeed broken. The doctors gave me the option of getting surgery to reset the bone or to let it heal on its own with a cast. I hated the idea of surgery so I opted to let it heal on its own. They brought out a cast, tightened it up on my finger, and sent me on my way. They gave me a time frame of about two months before it completely healed.

It was the last month of my lease for the apartment so I needed to get out. There were no solid jobs in Glassboro and I didn't have anywhere to stay in New York City. Plus, I didn't want to have the same scenario in which I got a menial job for a while until I realized I couldn't pay my bills.

Exploring all my options, I called my Uncle Mike in Chicago to see how he was doing. He said, "Why don't you come out here for a while to see if you like it?"

I thought it wasn't the worst idea. They lived in Evanston, a small suburb about an hour north of Chicago. I was born in Evanston and it'd be a change of scenery. The Versa was working fine so I'd be able to drive out there and have a car. After discussing it with my family, I decided to head out to the Midwest.

I printed out the directions and left for the ten-hour drive in the middle of the night. The trip was peaceful except for the shooting pain in my broken finger. I arrived the next morning and said hi to my 18-year-old cousin Nadine, who had just woken up.

My room was in the basement, since that was the only space they had free, but that was fine with me. I didn't know anybody in Evanston, so the experience turned out to be an informal rehab. I felt no pressure to drink and my diet consisted of turkey and cheese sandwiches.

One Saturday, my uncle asked me what book I was reading. I said, "Oh no, I don't read books."

Slightly agitated, he said, "You don't read books? Why not?"

"Oh they're just not my thing. They're boring."

"They may be boring at times, but I believe everybody should have a book they're in the middle of reading."

"Okay."

He looked at me with a skeptical eye, "Okay, there's a book that I want you to read. I really think you'll like it."

"What is it?"

"It's called <u>On The Road</u> by Jack Kerouac. I think you'd relate to it."

"Okay, I'll read this book…for you. Then I'll tell you what I think of it afterwards."

"Okay, that's perfect."

My days were free so I opened up the book and started reading. The writing was weird but I kept reading and actually started to like it. The main character was a guy who traveled across America, something I had just done. I read the book day and night until I finished. I told my uncle I enjoyed it. I wanted to read more, but only quality books.

Barely having any money, I went to the public library nearby and got a card. Skimming the books, I noticed <u>The Autobiography of Malcom X</u> by Alex Hayley. I knew Malcolm X was badass and thought it would be an interesting story. So I checked it out.

The story was so real, like I was standing right next to him during his experiences. At one point, he went to jail for a few years. Instead of wasting his time though, he read every book he could get his hands on. At that moment, I felt like Malcolm X. In Evanston I didn't know anybody, barely had any money, and didn't have a job. What I did have though was a library card. And for the rest of the summer I tried to be like Malcolm X, reading whatever I could get my hands on.

--

All day long, I read. I never realized how interesting reading could be until I actually did it.

After two months, my broken finger was nearly healed. I found a specialist nearby who removed the cast, but instructed me to keep a splint on so it stayed in place. He also told me to soak it in ice water every few hours to reduce the swelling, instructions I followed vehemently. It was such an annoying injury that I wanted it to heal as soon as possible.

Over time, the pain subsided and it started to function as an actual finger. To give me breaks from reading all day long and to get some exercise, I joined a gym, following the advice of the psychiatrist from Maine. It was such simple advice, but so powerful. It was amazing what happened when you spent a half hour to an hour pushing your body to the limit by working out.

The gym was a few miles from the house. Signing up, I was only hoping to run a little bit and lift weights. However, the guy said they had a full basketball court and a basketball league. When I looked at the court, I laughed. I felt like God was telling me, "Tyson, keep playing basketball."

In between reading, I'd trudge through the summer heat to the gym, get some shots up, then lift some weights, while getting my finger back to normal. I joined a league team, and playing basketball again felt amazing. I still had talent so I was easily one of the best players. Playing again got me thinking, *Was professional basketball a possibility?*

To find out, I called Rick one night.

"What's up Scooby Doo?? I wanna be like you when I grow up."

"What's up Rick?"

"You tell me big tiimmmeerrrrrr."

I laughed, "So my finger is healing and I'm destroying this competition in a gym league in Chicago. I still feel like I have the talent to play somewhere. I know you mentioned before about playing in Europe and I was wondering if that's still a possibility."

"Look man, you never played Division 1 and you only averaged 15 points per game at Division 3. It'll be hard to convince a team to pick you up with those stats."

"Yea, I know. But is it a possibility?"

"I don't know man, let me ask around. But keep working out and stay in shape."

"Ok, thanks a lot Rick."

"Word."

Slightly energized by the thought of playing basketball overseas, I made a renewed focus on training. I made sure to stay even more disciplined and began completely dominating the league games. Being realistic about my chances of playing pro ball though, I applied for jobs in the area just in case. On my resume I put together what shaky work experience I had at the time.

One job I interviewed for required walking door to door to sell products. I spent an entire day shadowing two employees. It was miserable and I decided I definitely didn't want to do that. At a FedEx store, one of the guys behind the counter did a basketball shooting motion with his hands. I thought, *Yea baby*, as I hoped Rick would come through.

Thinking it would help me get clarity, I searched for a psychiatrist. I found one, but she charged $80 per hour. I needed someone to talk to so I went. I told her my situation but she didn't provide much insight. When exactly sixty minutes passed, she said time was up. She told me it would take a few more sessions before she could get a good sense of my situation. Not knowing if she was genuine or just trying to take my money, I paid for the session but never went back.

--

As the summer came to a close, I still hadn't gone to court in Secaucus for the abandoned vehicle. I kept pushing it off month after month but I couldn't push it off anymore. I decided that late August was when I'd finally face the judge.

Living in Evanston helped me get my life back together, but I didn't see a future there. None of the jobs worked out, I didn't have any friends, and it wasn't too exciting. I told my aunt and uncle that going back to New Jersey would be my best move. They were sad but supported my decision. They wanted the best for me, wherever that was.

When I got back, I knew I had to keep my options open. Brainstorming with my mom and grandma, the idea of the military came up. I didn't want to get stuck behind a desk somewhere with a boring job, so I thought the military might be exciting. I was still in great shape and had an athletic background so I thought it might be a fit.

Researching the different factions of the military, I was drawn to the Navy SEALs. Watching documentaries about them when I was younger, I had huge amounts of respect for their training and abilities. They were the best of the best, and if I was going to join the military I was going to go all in.

I went to a recruiting station nearby and told the guy who I was and what my plans were. He was impressed I had a college degree, explaining I could start off as an officer making a decent salary. The salary was much more than I had made in the past few years.

To join, it was required I take a test called the ASVAB to figure out how smart I was. From there, they could place me in whatever I wanted to specialize in. He explained if I wanted to follow the SEAL path, getting a high score on the ASVAB was mandatory. They were warriors, but they were smart warriors.

Figuring out what the heck the ASVAB was, I went to Barnes and Noble and bought a training program for the test. I went through every section, taking the practice tests and studying all the information. On the day of the test, I scored a 96 out of 100, putting me in the top 1% of candidates.

When the recruiters found out my score, they were ecstatic. Since I was on the SEAL path, they hooked me up with a few other potential candidates who I'd be training with. One of the guys was actually in my homeroom in high school. For training, we went to a pool and worked on the sidestroke, which was the only stroke the SEALs used. For strength training, we did pushups, flutter kicks, pull-ups, and burpees. However, they constantly said physical strength didn't matter, only the strength of the mind. The guys who became SEALs weren't the strongest; they were the ones who never quit no matter what.

The trainers suggested I read a book that had recently come out, <u>Lone Survivor</u> by Marcus Luttrell. I checked it out from the library. What I read blew my mind. After finishing the final page, I vowed to never complain about anything again. Another book I noticed at the library was called <u>SEAL of Honor</u>, which detailed the life and death of Mike Murphy. Reading these books gave me an extreme sense of honor and solidified the thought that becoming a SEAL was something I wanted to do.

A day after training with the Navy guys, Rick called and said he might be able to hook me up with a basketball gig in Sweden. I was thrilled. He told me to send him my stats for the year and any video I had. I sent him everything I could.

The next day at the pool practicing my swimming times, I thought of two things. First, I realized that I hated swimming. I liked to be in the water, but long stretches of swimming made me miserable. Being a SEAL required long swims, over two miles at some points, and I didn't think I wanted to do that. For me it was just too boring and too lonely. I wasn't competing with anybody, it was just the same stroke, over and over and over again.

The second thought was something I read in SEAL of Honor. In BUD/S, the training program to become a SEAL, Mike Murphy almost lost both of his feet. There was a circulation problem from the intense training and the doctors almost went through with an amputation. At the last minute they didn't, but it was a close call. I thought, *Shit, I don't want to lose my feet. I like my feet.*

Regardless, the summer reached a crescendo until one of two things was going to happen: I'd either join the Navy or play professional basketball.

--

August 25, 2010 came, the day of my court appearance for the abandoned vehicle in Secaucus. Sweden was very close to happening but it wasn't solidified yet. Rick told me they were offering to pay for my plane ticket, they just needed to get the money together.

My mom drove me up to Secaucus for the afternoon court appearance. I arrived early, letting them know I was there. It was a large courtroom and my mom and I sat together in the back middle. Slowly, people began to file in until the room was full. We waited a while until the judge appeared.

"ALL RISE!"

We all stood up as the judge took her place at the helm.

She began, "For the first case of the day, the city of Secaucus versus Tyson

Hartnett!"

I thought, *Damn, I got the whole city against me?*

I meandered my way through the people to the spot in front.

"Tyson Hartnett?"

"Yes, ma'am."

"Is there anybody representing you today?"

"No, ma'am."

She detailed the charges against me and asked how I wanted to plead: Guilty or not guilty.

The judge continued, "If you plead not guilty, you will be assigned a lawyer and must come back another day to state your case. If you plead guilty, you must pay a $100 fine and lose your driver's license for a year. How do you plead?"

Shocked by what she just said, I thought, *Lose my license for a year?! For leaving my car outside?! What the hell?!* The silence weighed on the court-room as they waited for me to speak.

In about five seconds, I analyzed all my options. If I pleaded not guilty, which I felt, I would have to come back to Secaucus with a lawyer and state my case. Maybe they'd reduce the charge, but maybe not.

If I pleaded guilty, I'd only have to pay $100 and lose my license for a year. Banking on the fact that I might be going to Sweden to play professional basketball, I only needed my passport to get overseas, not the license.

She repeated her question, "What do you plead?"

I brought the microphone to my mouth and spoke, "Guilty, your honor."

"Okay, provide the security guard with your license and pay your fine at the office outside. NEXT!"

I walked away from the podium, past the stares of the crowd. I handed over my license and paid the lady in the window in the hall. I could tell by my mom's face that she was mad. She said the punishment was way too harsh for leaving my car parked outside. I tried to calm her down by saying there was nothing I could do about it anymore.

As we walked to the car outside, Rick called and said Sweden was a go. Basic training for the Navy started in November, and I didn't want to wait that long. Relieved that Sweden was definitely going to happen, he sent me the flight itinerary from New York City to Gothenburg. I said my goodbyes to my family and friends, getting ready to play my first season of professional basketball.

6
MY FIRST YEAR PLAYING
PRO BASKETBALL

When the plane touched down in Sweden, I thought, *This is it. Pro basketball, baby.* A lifelong dream was about to come true.

When I exited the plane I was surprised to see everything written in Swedish. I knew this was their country, but I was hoping for more English. Instead of reading the words, I followed the symbols to decipher where to go. Rick said someone from the team would be there to greet me, but I didn't know if they'd actually show up.

Walking past the security gate, I saw a guy sitting down who reminded me of Rick, with a basketball polo shirt on. I walked over to him as he stood up.

He outstretched his hand and said in a Swedish accent, "Hi... Tyson?"

"Yes, how are you?"

"Good, man. My name is Oleg, and this is Freddy."

He pointed at the younger guy next to him as I outstretched my hand, "I'm Tyson, nice to meet you."

"Same man, it's good to have you here."

I smiled, "Well it's great to be here."

We talked for a minute as Oleg directed us to the car. Then, we started the drive to Nassjo. The trip was three hours and I tried to sleep as much as I could. However, I kept waking up. I thought, *Tyson, you're in Sweden about to play professional basketball. Why would you go to sleep?*

The scenery outside the window was beautiful, with rolling hills and bright sun that made everything seem magical. I'd traveled all across America, but there was something different about those hills. I heard Rick's voice in the back of my head telling me I was there for business, not vacation, but I still wanted to appreciate the scenery.

Freddy and Oleg must have seen me try to rest because they kept asking me, "Are you tired?"

Each time, I replied, "Yes, very much." I didn't know how much English they spoke so I tried to keep it simple.

After three hours, we arrived in Nassjo, Sweden. The first thing I noticed were all the Swedish-looking houses I'd seen in movies. Then we passed the SportHallen where the games and practices were to be played.

Nearby, Oleg parked the car and led me to an apartment building. My room had an extra-long bed. There was a full kitchen, a living room with black leather couches, a desk, and a balcony. It was perfect.

After showing me around, Oleg said, "Hey, I have to go, but practice is in four hours. Do you remember where the gym is?"

"Yea, I think so."

"Okay, it's at the end of the road. Just follow the street and you'll make it there."

"Okay, great. Thanks so much, man."

After all this time I finally had my own apartment again…but I had to come all the way to Sweden to get it.

--

I unpacked and laid down for some rest, setting an alarm on my phone. I woke up a few hours later. With the time difference I had no idea what time it really was. Freaking out, I thought I missed practice. I thought, *Great Tyson, you missed your first practice. Now they're going to kick you off the team and send you home.*

I frantically packed up my basketball clothes and threw my sweatshirt on. It wasn't freezing outside yet, but I quickly learned that it was cold enough in mid-September to warrant heavier clothes. Remembering Oleg's words, *"At the end of the road,"* I turned right. If only the road were yellow with bricks, I would have felt like Dorothy from the Wizard of Oz.

After about fifteen minutes of walking, the road intersected with a larger, heavier trafficked street. On the opposite side was the SportHallen, so I was relieved.

Inside the SportHallen, multiple trophy cases lined the hallway. One of the rooms off to the side provided tea and coffee. Nobody was around so I started checking the place out. The doors to the gym were locked, which I took as a good sign that I hadn't missed practice.

After about twenty minutes of poking around the building, Oleg showed up. He said, "Hey Tyson, what are you doing here so early?"

I replied, "I fell asleep and have no idea what time it is, so I came over. Did I miss practice?"

He laughed, "No, practice starts in an hour. I'll open up the gym now for you though, if you want to shoot."

"Okay, that'd be great."

He unlocked the doors to the gym and I followed him in.

On both sides of the court sat bleachers that went up about six rows. Soccer nets behind the hoops provided a storage area for extra items. Advertisements for local businesses lined the walls, all in Swedish. The gym was outlined in green, since that was Nassjo Basket's team colors.

Like back in Maine before early morning practices, I loved the sight of an open gym. To me, it was pure. The hoops didn't judge you, and the lines of the court meant opportunity...opportunity to sweat and put myself through an intense workout, which would only pay off in the future. In an open gym, it was me versus myself. Only I determined the work I put in and only I determined my destiny.

Oleg got me a ball from behind the soccer net and I started to dribble. It was an official FIBA ball, the ball which all the professional teams in Europe use. I took a few shots as Oleg walked back out into the lobby. He left me all alone in a gym in the middle of Sweden, and everything at that moment felt right.

Twenty minutes later, my teammates started showing up. I was expecting massive 6'6" to 6'10" guys with muscles on top of muscles, but I saw the opposite. Every teammate that walked in looked like a hipster from Brooklyn. Many of them were skinny, with blonde hair and poignant blue eyes. Expecting to be one of the smallest players on the team, I actually turned out to be one of the biggest. I didn't mind it, as long as every other team in the league was the same way. I could guard seven-foot players, but didn't prefer it. Everybody I met was very nice.

In the back of the gym was a door that led down a creaky spiral staircase to the basement. In the basement was the locker room and a weight-lifting area down the hall. They told me where my locker was and I got dressed for practice.

Back on the court, the coaches made introductions. I was polite and I could tell they were excited to have an American on the team.

When practice started, we began with warmups and drills. There were a few differences from what I was used to, but it wasn't dramatic. I kept thinking, *Am I as good as these guys, or are they going to be much better than me?*

When the coaches split up the teams to start the games, that's when I found out for certain. After we had played for five minutes I knew I was a better player. They were all solid, but with my years and years of knowledge about the game, I scored on nearly any defender. On defense, I knew how to defend against all the feints they tried against me. Since I was as strong or stronger, they couldn't push me around.

Once I figured this out, I breathed a sigh of relief that I wasn't going to get my ass handed to me every day. Thinking about how Rick said I needed to average at least twenty points per game, I now saw that as a possibility. If I felt overmatched like back in Maine, there'd be no way I could score twenty a game.

By the end of the first practice, everybody in the gym knew I was a great player. The coaches saw it and my teammates knew I was solid. This was important because I needed them to see me as an asset instead of a liability. If they didn't think I was good, they wouldn't pass me the ball and then I wouldn't be able to take shots and score.

After practice, we all went into the locker room to get changed. To my surprise, they all spoke Swedish. In locker rooms throughout my life I wouldn't say much, but I could at least understand what everybody else was saying. Here, I had absolutely no idea. The more they talked, the funnier this foreign language seemed to me. When they looked at me I just smiled and nodded, having no idea what they were saying.

A few of the guys walked me back to the apartment. So far I liked these guys and they seemed to like me, so we were off to a great start. We hung out at the apartment for a few minutes. When they finally left, I was all alone in Nassjo, Sweden on my first day playing professional basketball.

I didn't know what the future held, but so far it seemed promising.

--

Playing professional basketball, I thought everybody would be so excited and want to know every detail. In reality, I only received one email a few days after I arrived in Nassjo. It was from my dad saying, "How's it going?"

I realized that yes, I was playing professional basketball, but everybody still had their own lives. I messaged a few people on Facebook but they were only somewhat interested in what was happening. They had their lives and I had mine.

There was no food in the apartment so I went to the supermarket to find something to eat. I stuck to the basics like cereal, pizzas, and anything else that took a few minutes to heat up. There was no microwave so I used the stove for heating.

I was the only American and I didn't have a roommate for the first month. I was by myself without a laptop or working cell phone in a cold apartment in Nassjo. At times my teammates came by to hang out, but they also had their own lives.

When the first weekend came, the team invited me out to Jonkoping, a larger city twenty minutes away, to party with them. We went to a teammate's house to drink lots of alcohol and listen to epic Swedish music. Eventually, a teammate pulled out a bottle of Brooklyn Vodka that he had bought in America. We all took shots, shouting, "BROOKLYNNNN!"

Towards the end of the night, when we were all sufficiently drunk, someone suggested we go to the bar. I had no idea what was happening so I just followed the person in front of me.

Later that night I got separated from the guys and found myself all alone at the edge of a river. In the distance I saw a bridge and wondered if I should try to swim to the other side. Nearby was a canoe but it was tied down with a heavy rope that I couldn't budge.

Thinking that fording the river was my only option, I waded into the water. As the coldness clutched my ankles I remembered I had my passport in my pocket. I didn't want to ruin it, so I slowly backed out. For some reason I was completely determined to cross the river, but I was also exhausted from the alcohol. I told myself I'd take a nap to regain my strength, then try to conquer it in a few hours. I laid down on a nearby bench and closed my eyes.

Sunlight woke me a few hours later. I wondered where the heck I was. Feeling sick, I walked toward the street. I had no phone and no idea which direction I should head, but I thought the cars would help me. I put my thumb up, hoping I'd be able to hitchhike back to Nassjo and the warmth of the apartment. After ten cars passed without stopping, I decided it was futile.

But then a taxi came by a few minutes later and I flagged it down. I spoke no Swedish, but said, "Nassjo?"

He replied in broken English, "Four hundred kroner."

Four hundred kroner translated to about $60, and I wasn't going to spend that much to get back to the apartment. I replied, "Ok, no tack," which translated to, "No thank you."

He nodded and drove off.

Feeling completely helpless and lost, I kicked myself for not staying around the guys the night before. I couldn't be too angry since I couldn't even remember anything that happened. All I knew was that I was cold, nauseous, and completely alone.

I put my hands in my pockets to keep them from the brisk air of the Swedish morning. In my left hand I felt a piece of paper. It was a phone number with a name on it. Elated that I had some sort of contact, I followed the road to a gas station in the distance. Without finding this piece of paper, I would have been wandering around Jonkoping for hours.

At the gas station, I asked the attendant to call the number. Fortunately, someone picked up on the other end and they conversed in Swedish for a few seconds. The attendant said to me, "What's your name?"

"Tyson."

She repeated it, spoke some more Swedish, then hung up. Providing a map from behind the counter, she detailed the direction for me to head. I thanked her and started walking.

Arriving at the location, I spotted my teammate James on the balcony of an apartment. He shouted, "Tyson!"

Extremely relieved to see him, I said, "Jamessss!! What's up man!! You saved my life bro!"

He laughed and said, "I'll be right down!"

I gave him a hug when I saw him and we went up to the apartment. I explained to him what happened and he just laughed again. He said everybody got completely wasted and Freddy slept outside too, so I wasn't the only one. He gave me some orange juice and let me sleep on his couch in the warmth, while we waited to return to Nassjo later that day.

--

When the week started up again, I felt the honeymoon wearing off. The excitement that I was there started to die down. Now, it was about performing on the court so we could win games.

Trying to figure out things to do other than basketball, I asked Oleg if I could be useful for anything else. He replied, "Well, it's mandatory that you coach our younger team, and if you want, you can go to the school and play basketball with the younger kids when they're not in class."

I think he was telling me I was there for one reason and one reason only: To play and win basketball games. If I had other hobbies, that was great, but my number one priority was to perform during the games. Everything else was secondary.

Still without a laptop, I needed to get connected to the outside world. James told me about OnOff, a Swedish store that sold computers. I walked over there and picked out the cheapest laptop they had, an eMachine for 3,500 Swedish kroner ($500). The keys were in Swedish and it's the same computer I'm using to type these words, four years later. Back then, I knew I wouldn't need it for much, only Skype, e-mail, and checking the internet.

Here's a few things I observed during my first few weeks in Nassjo:

- It was a quaint town, with only two streets of shops and restaurants. The rest of the area was houses. The town rested on the west side of Sweden, about six hours from Stockholm.

- Oleg gave me coupons for free food from different pizza places. Sometimes I ate at the shop, and it was cool to be around the locals. Most of them spoke little English, so I could rarely understand what they were saying to me. But a few would talk to me about Obama, America, and what they thought of the world. I loved getting an outsider's perspective on America, especially someone who lived deep in Sweden.

- I could never read the newspaper since it was in Swedish, but I always turned to the back to check out the weather across the world. I noticed when it was 30 degrees in New York, while it was typically 75 in Los Angeles. Considering I was making my way through feet of snow every day, I would have done anything to be in 75 degree weather. Then I would think about how far I actually was from Los Angeles. This wasn't the other side of the country in Maine… it was the other side of the *world*.

- The guys in the locker room would rarely cover up. In the states, some guys showered with their underwear on, uncomfortable being naked. Here, guys stood right next to each other buck naked. I knew if anybody tried that in America, they'd probably get knocked out.

- The communication in the locker room was hard. I was never the most outspoken guy, but I could usually chip in lines here and there, flowing with the conversation. When guys are speaking a completely different language though, it's impossible. I could only nod and smile. If someone addressed me, they'd have to translate, which would ruin the flow of conversation. This kept me out of a lot of banter, which I think added to my feelings of seclusion. I tried to learn as much Swedish as possible, but it's a hard language.

- Two words: Swedish MTV.

- The candy was amazing. I had never eaten better candy in my life, and wondered how the young kids kept all their teeth. The movie store not only had DVD's, but also a huge rack of nearly a hundred different kinds of candy and chocolate. It was a buffet, so I'd get a bag, fill it up, then pay by weight. I got a bag every single week. I even sent a bag to a friend in America.

--

As for basketball, the reason I was there, I quickly positioned myself as the best player on the team. Rick kept pounding into my head, "You have to average at least 20 points and win every game. If you don't do that, they'll send you home and bring in another American."

My first professional basketball game was against a team in Jonkoping, a town twenty minutes away from Nassjo. Wanting to prove myself, I was determined to score at least 20 points. We took the bus to the game, got changed, and started the typical warmup routine. In warmups, a really weird electronic song called "We No Speak Americano" played over the loudspeakers. I thought, *What the hell is this? I'm definitely not in America anymore.*

Expecting thousands of fans to be in the stands chanting, I was surprised that it was quite different. The gym was small, with only about 100 people in attendance, most of them families of the players. It reminded me of the fans at Rowan, who were mostly there to watch their friends and family, not the passionate fans who'd camp out for hours before the hockey games at Maine.

When the game started, it took me a few minutes to get accustomed to the style of play, but then I turned on my skills. I hit shots, played great defense, and even made a defender fall at one point. In the second half I played even better, finding my rhythm as I passed and scored at will. At the end of the game, we won by about ten points, which was the perfect scenario for my first game. Receiving the stats for the game, I had 20 points, 10 rebounds, and a few assists. Knowing I played solid defense as well, it was a perfect start to the season. I was proud of myself and knew there was more to come. I also proved to the team that this American was a solid investment.

My teammates congratulated me and I appreciated their love, hoping that it would continue throughout the season. I called Rick and my dad when I got back to the apartment and they were both happy for me. In typical fashion though, they told me not to rest, and to do it again the next game.

Every game from then on, my mission was to score at least 20 points. Even if we were winning, I still had to do my part. They brought me in for a reason, and if I didn't perform they could easily bring in another player to take my spot. I didn't want that, so I did anything I could to prove myself.

With this mindset, I cared about my teammates but I wasn't there to make friends. I was there to bust the other team's ass by scoring points and winning games. The dichotomy here was that many of my teammates played basketball for fun. My roommate had a full-time job working for a Swedish finance company and most of my other teammates were full-time students. They played part time, but didn't put in the intense extra work that I typically would.

This intense work actually got me into trouble. One day at practice a teammate who rarely showed up was on my team, and he didn't move out of the way when I told him to. I had the ball on the wing and he just stood there. I shouted to him again, "Move!"

Instead of moving, he just stopped playing, looking at me with an expression that said, "No. Don't tell me what to do."

I never had a teammate who just stopped playing, so I didn't know how to react. I screamed at him again to move, but he stayed still. Eventually, I said, "What the fuck are you doing?"

When I said that, he got angry and replied in his Swedish accent, "What the fuck am *I* doing? What the fuck are *you* doing? Who are *you*??"

Surprised, but not one to back down, I dropped the ball and walked over to him so we were standing face to face. I said, "You got a problem man?"

"Yea man, I do. You!"

I pushed him. All the other players crowded around and broke us up. I looked at him in disgust, knowing he never worked hard but was now trying to tell me how to play basketball. Honestly, it wasn't about him at all, I just wanted him to move to the freaking hoop.

In hindsight, this was the worst possible thing I could have done. In an altercation like this, who do you think the rest of the team will side with? Their friend who they grew up playing basketball with? Or the scary American who curses at their friend? I was doomed.

The next day at practice I said sorry to him in front of the team and he accepted, but the damage was done. Subtly, my teammates started to treat me differently. One day before practice, we were warming up, and I was shooting all by myself on one side of the court. When the rest of the team arrived, they all shot at the same hoop, but not one person came to my end to shoot with me. This was subtle, but powerful. Ten guys all shooting at the same basket, while one guy shoots at the other? That's a problem. After the altercation, they didn't want to be around me, and I knew it.

After that I tried to focus my energy on training and coaching the younger players. These kids were about twelve years old and only understood a little basketball. I ran them through basic drills and they picked it up pretty well. Most of them only spoke a little English though, so I had to speak slow and enunciate.

One of the kids, Anton, became one of my best friends during my entire time in Sweden. In practice he worked the hardest, translated my English when necessary, and took everything seriously. I appreciated this and he impressed me.

Even though I was intense, I knew when to laugh. One of the best moments during my time in Sweden came when I was warming up the younger guys with pushups and sit-ups before practice. When we crowded around, Anton said things to me like, "Bog" and "Fitta." All the other players laughed and I just smiled and nodded with them. When I did this, they laughed even harder.

After training one day, I asked Anton why they laughed so much. He said, "I'm saying 'You are very ugly' and 'You are a mother fucker.'"

When I heard this, I started laughing with him.

--

Living in Nassjo, Sweden, loneliness sometimes kicked into high gear. To alleviate this, I Skyped my friends and family, even writing letters sometimes. When I told Rick about being lonely, he replied, "Look man, I've got guys in Siberia with no internet or phone. They just count their money all day. You're playing pro basketball. This is what it's like. Count your money and be grateful."

I took his advice and counted my money, but since I wasn't getting paid that much it only took me about two minutes to count.

Here's the thing about professional basketball. Many people think it's a glamorous lifestyle with fame and money. Maybe in some parts of the world it is, but not everywhere. For a lot of guys playing overseas, it's the same thing day after day, week after week, month after month.

A Day in the Life

The alarm goes off at 9:00 AM and I reach over to shut it off. I immediately remember I'm in Sweden and think, *Here we go…another day in Sweden.*

Today we only have a practice since we play one game per week, typically on the weekends. The rest of the week is free time, and for me that means lots of reading and weight lifting. I asked Oleg once if I could get a job somewhere, but not knowing Swedish was a huge barrier. It was cute that I played basketball, but no business was going to trust an American to work for them who spoke zero Swedish. They were in business to make money, not to risk their profit with some American.

I sit up on the side of the bed and look at the snow resting on the tree-tops outside. It's beautiful, but it's also cold. I get up and walk to the kitchen, pouring myself some cereal. I bring the bowl to the desk in the living room and open up the laptop. My Swedish roommate and teammate is already gone for the day, working his day job, so I'm all alone once again.

Opening my email and Facebook, I see the same news going on in the world. Nothing's mind-blowing or surprising so I close the laptop and go back to my room. I bundle up with clothes, getting ready to walk to the SportHallen to lift weights.

Slipping on the shoes my teammate lent me, I put on the heavy jacket my dad sent in the mail a few weeks ago. I power up my iPod, starting the day with the new Kanye West album. I put in my earbuds, grab my bag, and walk outside.

Making the same walk and doing the same routine every single day gets old, but I'm a professional basketball player, right? Arriving at the SportHallen, I change in the locker room. The weight room is actually impressive, with dumbbells going up to 150 pounds and an expansive array of weight machines, squat racks, and benches.

Today is my back and biceps day, so I do three exercises of each muscle group. The Swedish Kilos messed me up to start, but after a few days I figured out the conversions. While there are normally not many people in the weight room, today there is a massive weightlifter doing squats in the back. He has an Olympic-style weight belt on and is doing 800-pound sets.

In between my bicep curls, he notices me resting until the next set. He speaks up, "Hej, helppa?" I nod and walk over without saying a word, not wanting to seem like an ignorant American who doesn't speak Swedish.

He has a partner who guides the weights on the left side while I stand guard on his right. He puts the 800 pounds on his neck, pumps out a few reps, then strains on the final one as I help place the bar back onto the rack.

He looks at me and says, "Mycket tack." (Thank you.)

I nod and respond with one of the only Swedish words I know. "Valkommen." (You're welcome.)

I finish up my workout then go back to the locker room, where I bundle up again, ready to make my way to a restaurant for lunch.

I trudge through the snow to the restaurant I ate at yesterday, and the day before that, and the day before that. Being part of the Nassjo basketball team, I'm allowed to eat a free meal every day from the restaurant. They have white table cloths, a salad bar, and a buffet in the back. Being 6'6" and hungry, nothing can beat this place.

I eat as I listen to some new music on my iPod, soaking in the sights and sounds around me. At a table nearby there are a few businessmen speaking Swedish. At another table, there's an elderly couple. I realize that it doesn't matter if I'm in Chicago, Maine, New Jersey, or Sweden, people live similar lives, only in different locations.

Once I finish eating, I get up and leave. Freddy told me that there's no reason to tip, and it's not encouraged. It's actually slightly disrespectful here, so I don't leave any money. I walk back to the apartment with plans to travel to Jonkoping to bring back some library books.

Getting to Jonkoping is easy and it's a respite from the monotony of Nassjo. It's only about twenty minutes away, and as the train pulls into the station the huge lake appears outside the window. Swedish houses dot the valley bordering the lake, forming a 'V' shape with the point at the train station. There's snow on the ground and it's quite beautiful.

I get off the train and head down the main street of shops, which is much more vibrant than Nassjo and gets me energized. I think, *Maybe all of Sweden isn't boring, maybe I'm just in the wrong city*.

Nearing the library, I see the large bridge in the distance. The same bridge I tried to ford the night after the party, I was glad I didn't attempt that since I probably would have drowned.

The front of the library looks similar to every one I'd ever been to, only all the writing is in Swedish. I head upstairs for the section of English books. The options aren't quality bestsellers, but it's enough to keep my mind working. I choose a few that I think will be interesting during the long, dark nights.

I've got nothing else to do in Jonkoping, plus I have practice later in the day, so I go back to the train station. Staring out at the lake in front of me, the sting of loneliness hits me hard. I wish I could just get into a boat and paddle my way back to America, where I've got friends and family. Then I realize that if I started paddling up that lake it would actually take me deeper into Sweden. I take a deep breath, put the thought out of my head, and open up one of the books as the train approaches.

Back in Nassjo, I rest up for a few hours until practice starts. Some days I'll write a letter to someone back home, but today I just want to rest. An hour before practice, I start to get ready. Memories from Maine still in my mind, I feel anxious and nervous for practice. I don't feel terrified I'll never play on the team, but it's a feeling that says, *Perform, otherwise your dreams of playing professional basketball will be over with.*

At the gym, I see the younger teams' practice wrapping up. I make my way to the locker room as some guys are already getting changed. Once dressed, I go to the court and get warm.

When everybody arrives, Coach Mats brings us all together to discuss the plan for practice. We start with warmup drills, then transition into stretching. After stretching, we shoot, run plays, and eventually scrimmage. To finish practice, we perform a drill where every miss is minus two with every make plus one. The goal is to get to plus 10. If we get to negative 10, we have to start the drill all over again.

Today, nobody makes their shots as we hit negative 10 a few times in a row. Frustrated, Coach Mats says, "Ok, rules are changed. For every make, it's plus two, for every miss it's minus one."

We hit plus ten easily, but this makes me mad. In America, the coach would never just change the rules in the middle of the drill. They would make us run and run until we achieved plus 10. Even in my own practices, I'd never change the rules. I'd be in the gym for four hours until I achieved plus 10. Switching the rules is blasphemy, yet nobody said anything about it. *(Editor's note: I recently asked Coach Mats about this and he said, "I'm sure I did that, but I was tired and wanted to go home. I was working 45 hours per week at the University, then 25 hours a week coaching the team. I was most likely exhausted. That would have never happened when I was a player though. No way.")*

After we hit plus 10, we stretch some more then go back down into the locker room. We all go our separate ways, since most of the guys have girlfriends or families to spend time with. I told Anton that I'd eat with him after practice, so he is waiting for me outside.

We walk over to the burger shop and I use the free coupon Oleg gave me for the burgers. I chat with Anton about life. His parents recently got divorced, so we can relate to each other. He's only 12 years old but he's my best friend in Sweden. We laugh, make fun of each other, and talk about the NBA. He loves Kobe Bryant, but I tell him Kobe doesn't even compare to Michael Jordan.

Looking out the window at the snow-covered road, I experience an intense sensation of deja-vu, like I've been in the burger shop before. Thinking about it, it's not deja-vu at all, but what I pictured Sweden would look like when I was back in New Jersey.

When we finish eating, I accompany Anton back to his house. After that, I walk back to my apartment to eat some candy and read until I fall asleep. Tomorrow will be extremely similar, as will the day after that.

--

As games continued, we racked up the wins and I racked up the points. I averaged about 18 points per game with 8 rebounds. Ten games into the season, we had lost only one game. Even though it was boring for me during the days, I was still performing on the court. They may not have liked me, but they couldn't argue with stats. Whether we had a home game or an away game, I consistently produced, just like they wanted me to. For that, I was proud of myself.

Nearing Christmas break, Oleg wanted to talk to me before practice one day. I figured it would be about the holiday travel plans since I was flying back to America for the break. I showed up at the gym an hour early and waited for him outside. When he arrived, he brought me into the coffee shop with Coach Mats.

"Tyson, you're doing great, we're winning games, and you're a tough player," Oleg said. "I like that."

Thinking they were going to give me a raise, I replied, "Thanks Oleg, I appreciate it."

He nodded. "Unfortunately though, we're going to be bringing in a different American."

Not understanding what he was saying, I said, "That's a good thing, right? Two Americans are better than one."

"No, he will be taking your place on the team."

Still not understanding, I said, "What do you mean, he'll be taking my room?"

"No, he'll be taking your spot on the team."

I was silent as what he was saying finally started to sink in. My heart rate soared and my mind searched for answers. "Wait, what? You're kicking me off the team?"

"Yes, we have decided a new American would be the best fit for the team."

Stunned, shocked, and not knowing what to do, I replied, "Why? I'm the leading scorer and we have a great record."

He explained that the players didn't think I fit in with them, and they didn't like my attitude. He kept talking but I stopped listening.

My worst nightmare was coming true.

I sat there and asked him a few more questions. Trying to control my emotions, there was nothing I could say or do to change his mind.

Towards the end, he said, "Also Tyson, there are two more games left. I expect you to be a professional about this. Can you do that?"

With no choice, I replied, "Yes, I can do that."

"Okay, good." We stood up and shook hands, and I went into the locker room to get ready for practice.

I practiced but I was still in shock. All the work, sacrifice, and loneliness was just so I could get kicked off of the team at Christmas time. Knowing that Rick would curse me out for twenty minutes when he found out, I dreaded the conversation. In my mind, this was the worst possible scenario. We had a great record and I was averaging about 20 points per game, so it made no sense.

For the final two games until I left, I kept my word to Oleg and acted as a professional. I did my job, trained with the team, and got along with the guys, but I was a walking ghost. When I called Rick, he already knew, and told me to call Demetrius, who was the head coach of Brahe Basket in Jonkoping. Demetrius was from New Jersey like me but he had been coaching in Sweden for over ten years.

Demetrius said they would love to have me on the team once the holidays were finished. That got me excited that my hoop dreams weren't over with yet. Jonkoping was a bigger city anyway, so I thought it might be a good situation for me.

Before I signed to Brahe, they wanted to interview me to see if I'd fit in with the team. Rick told me not to mess this up, since it might be my last chance to play professional basketball. I went and charmed the pants off the president and another director. Afterwards, they said they really liked me and wanted me on the team. We didn't discuss money though.

When I told Oleg about possibly playing for Brahe, he said matter-of-factly, "They can't pay you a dime, but good luck."

After one of the last practices of the year, Coach Mats got the team together and told them that I'd be leaving. He explained it in Swedish so I didn't understand anything he said, but I looked around to get a sense of my teammates' reactions. Like I thought, nobody cared. Only one or two guys came up to me afterwards and said, "Hey Tyson, I'm sorry to see you go."

In the last game of the season, I had about twenty points but we lost. In the locker room after the game, everybody was quiet and I was ready to get the hell out of there. As the rest of my teammates sulked about the loss, I quickly got dressed, removed the picture from my locker, and walked out without saying bye to anybody. I'd probably never see any of them again, but they didn't want me there anyway. I walked back to my apartment, where I got ready to leave for America.

Anton was sad I was leaving and didn't understand the situation either. Before I left though, I made sure we exchanged gifts. He gave me a bottle of aftershave that I still have to this day. I sparingly use it, holding onto the memories of the gift.

On the day of my flight back to America, a storm surrounded all of Europe. It forced me to spend a day in Germany. There, I called my mom and sister, excited to come back to Marlton for Christmas. At the airport the next day, I created a mixtape for my sister of all the best songs I discovered while in Sweden. When it was my time for the flight, I got on the plane and headed back to America.

--

In Marlton, I analyzed the whole situation. In reality, I didn't like Nassjo anyway and was kind of glad they kicked me off the team. It was just too boring. I did the same things every day and didn't feel challenged intellectually. Even on the court I was much better than the other players. Trying to figure out *why* they kicked me off the team though was when it all made sense.

The reason was that I wasn't their ideal teammate. I didn't hang with the guys or join them in team activities. With the younger team that I coached, I didn't even travel to their away games. All I did was spend time in the apartment, reading books or on the computer.

I realized that when a team brings in an American, they want them to perform on the court, but they also want to learn about them off the court. They want to know about America, where the player grew up, and what they do for fun. Many times they'll see an American as this exotic creature from a foreign land, only hearing about what it's like in New York City or New Jersey, never able to actually go there. My downfall was being closed off and not getting them excited about me being on the team. I could have scored 50 points per game but if they didn't like me, it would have still been the same outcome. Unfortunately, this was a lesson I had to learn the hard way.

Yes, playing professional basketball was nice, but it wasn't anything like I thought it would be. It was college basketball all over again, only without the classes, girls, friends, and English-speaking people.

Christmas came and went and I got in touch with one of my new teammates on Facebook. He told me he'd pick me up when I got to Jonkoping, only I should take a train to Husqvarna, which was closer to his house. I didn't know where I'd be living yet but hoped we could make it work.

When I got to Husqvarna, standing alone in the cold with two big bags, I had a sinking feeling that this wasn't going to work out. There was no welcoming committee.

In time, Johan showed up with a few other teammates in a small, beat up car. One lesson from Rick that always stuck with me was to bring only one bag. Going on tournaments to Vegas and LA back in high school, if we had more than one bag, he would have more than likely sent us home. All we needed was the essentials, nothing more.

When I asked Johan where I'd be staying, he told me I'd live with him for a few days while the team figured it out. I thought, *Oh great, I'm homeless again.*

At least in Nassjo they had a setup for me to sleep and eat. That's all I needed because I knew I was there for business. But in Jonkoping I didn't even have my own place and everything was still up in the air. I didn't even know if I was going to get paid. At Johan's apartment, I met his roommate, who showed me the futon in the corner of his room.

At practice the next day, I learned that the entire team was full of teenagers, many of whom played basketball for fun. From what I saw, none of them took basketball as seriously as I did. One day in the weight room, one of the guys was doing calf raises on a machine in a sweater, just going through the motions. Another time doing sprints, I ran my hardest while they took it easy.

As time went on, it felt like there was little structure to what we did. Practices were spread out throughout the week, sometimes being cancelled if other people were using the gym. There were no outdoor courts or recreation centers, so we'd just have to go back to the apartment without working out. Training was the only thing I looked forward to, so when we couldn't practice it was a huge letdown.

In terms of my salary, I found out that they in fact could not pay me. They provided coupons for pizza or sandwiches in the city, but other than that I was on my own. Someone mentioned I could get a job in the city to make money. I thought, *If I wanted a job, I'd do it back in America, not in Jonkoping, Sweden.*

Eventually I moved out of Johan's apartment and in with Demetrius, the coach of Brahe from New Jersey. On the surface, I thought it would be great living with him since he spoke English. However, he was busy with a wife and kids, on top of his role as coach.

After two weeks in Jonkoping, I knew I needed to go back to America.

One day after practice, Demetrius drove me to his house. When he pulled in and parked the car, I said, "Mete, I think I should go back to America. This isn't working out here."

Expecting, even hoping, him to persuade me to stay, he instead replied, "Oh, that's too bad. I'll tell the president tomorrow."

He probably saw that the situation wasn't working out either, but there was nothing he could do about it. He didn't control the paychecks, the team did. The following day, the team bought me a one-way ticket back to New York City. Since I barely had any money, I remembered that Oleg mentioned before that Nassjo would pay me an extra month of salary for kicking me off the team. I messaged him and asked if I could pick that up before I went back to the states. He told me to come over the next day.

When I went to Nassjo for the last time to pick up the money, the finance director handed me an envelope. She had a weird look on her face that I read as, "Here you go, jerk."

That night I called my dad, then Rick, to tell them I was coming back to the states. I knew they were disappointed, but there was nothing I could do. My dad mentioned I could stay with him in New York while I searched for a job. My mom was living in Delaware and since I didn't have a license that was out of the question. In New York, I wouldn't need a car and there was more opportunity anyway.

On the day of the flight I had to take the train to the airport. I gave myself about an hour to get to the train, since I thought it was only about fifteen minutes away in a car. When I called for a taxi, all of them said it would take over an hour to get there. I was screwed, since I needed to catch this exact train to get to the flight on time. Demetrius wasn't home, so I put my bag over my back and started walking.

After a few minutes of trudging along the ice-covered road, a car approached. Mete rolled down the window and said, "Hey man, where you going?"

Relieved to see him, I replied, "To the train so I can catch the flight. Can you give me a ride?"

"Yea, sure."

Thankful that he came when he did, I got in. At the station, I shook his massive hand and we said goodbye.

I got onto the train and caught my flight back to America.

7
A CALLING

In New York, I slept on my dad's couch and felt like a complete failure once again.

I knew that I messed up in Sweden, wishing I could have at least stayed the entire season. If I had averaged 20 points per game throughout the year, I could have probably upgraded to a better town and team. Instead, they kicked me off halfway through, which meant no team would touch me.

When I talked to Rick, he told me, "Great job Tyson, you fucked up. This was your one shot. Do you know how many guys would kill to be in your shoes and have the chance to play professional basketball? All you had to do was smile, score points, and win games. That's it. But no, you couldn't even do that.

"I'm going to tell you this right now. You will never play in Europe again. I got you this job, and it was on you to establish a reputation for yourself. The way I see it, you're toast. If I tell any team to look at you, they're going to ask where you played before. I'll have to be honest and tell them that you averaged only 20 points per game in the lowest league in Sweden. When they contact the team, they will explain that they kicked you off because of your attitude. Do you think any team will touch you then?

"You never played at Maine, then you averaged 15 points per game at a small Division 3 school. Looking at your highlights, you aren't dunking in any of them. It's just basic highlights that anybody can do. It's not impressive. Who do you think a team will choose, a guy averaging 10 points per game at a Division 1 school who's dunking in his highlights, or a guy who averaged 15 points at a Division 3 school who got kicked off his team halfway through the year? You tell me.

"You blew it man. You blew it."

My hoop dreams felt over. I thought there was a small chance I might play somewhere the following season but it wasn't looking good. It was unclear if I'd ever be able to play professionally again. So I thought, *I might as well just get a job now.*

The thing about regret is that it can eat you alive. You can replay situations over and over in your mind, wondering about different possible outcomes. Looking at the Sweden situation, I got a lot of flak from Rick, but I didn't have any regrets. I stayed disciplined, worked my butt off and did what I could to fit in. But I definitely could have been more social.

In terms of basketball, I didn't have any regrets because I played my game. Some games I'd have more points than others, but I was always prepared. That's why when Rick made me feel terrible about what happened, I listened to him but also knew in my heart that I did everything I could. I'd learn from the situation, and that was it.

In New York I started applying to dozens of places every day. After nothing panned out, my dad introduced me to a guy who had a non-profit startup. He needed an assistant. I was fine with it since I needed some structure and money.

At that time I found something online that rubbed salt in the wound of not playing pro basketball anymore. It was the blog of the player who replaced me in Sweden. He was a 6'6" guy from Minnesota who had blonde hair, just like all the team members. Every few days he'd update the blog, saying things like, "I'm so lucky to be here," and, "This is my dream come true." In a painful, self-deprecating exercise, I read every word of his blogs, each sentence making me feel even worse about having my own dreams taken away.

In New York I needed to work out so I tried free passes at a bunch of different gyms. One of them was the Reebok Sports Club, an expensive gym with two full basketball courts. When I played pickup one night, it felt amazing to get back onto the court. I proved to everybody there I was a great player. However, once the games ended, I sat down with my back against the wall on the sideline. I thought, *Look at you. Yea, you can destroy this competition, but these guys are scrubs. You should be playing like this overseas. Great job.*

Not wanting to live on my dad's couch forever, I searched around for apartments on Craigslist. I found one in Jersey City for a decent price and immediately signed for it. The apartment was a high-rise overlooking the river, although my room was tucked deep in the middle and didn't have any windows. I wasn't crazy about that but I was desperate. My dad told me he'd help me pay for it since I barely had any money.

Looking for things to do outside of work, I messaged *Dime Magazine*, a basketball publication I read growing up, to see if they knew where to find games. After a week they got back to me, introducing me through email to Bobbito Garcia, a New York City streetball legend. I remembered Bobbito from the And1 Basketball Highlight Tapes, the *NBA Street* video game, a Nike Basketball commercial, and his own instructional videos, Bobbito's Basics to Boogie.

I was star-struck, hoping I wouldn't mess this up.

Here was my initial email to him:

Mr. Bobbito Garcia,

My name is Tyson Hartnett and I recently got back from playing basketball overseas. I was wondering if you knew of any good summer leagues in the New York City area. I emailed Dime Magazine, and they told me to email you because you, for sure, would be able to help me.

I am 24 years old and have a Business Management degree from Rowan University in New Jersey. I am living in Jersey City for the summer, and I don't know of any competitive leagues, except for the NY Urban League which is extremely expensive.

Also, I have an interest in writing, and thought maybe I could contribute to your magazine by describing the playground atmosphere in New York City during the summer time. I have recently been writing grants and believe I could write some articles about the different summer leagues or playgrounds. I could provide a unique perspective, especially coming from a 6'6" white guy. I have attached the correspondence I have had with

Dimemag at the end of this email.

Thanks for your time, and please let me know if you have any information on any summer leagues or if we can work together.

Talk to you soon,

A day later, Bobbito responded by telling me he'd put me on his open run email list. Messages included a time and location and whoever was available showed up to play. To me it sounded like heaven, so I thanked him profusely.

When I received my first open run email, I got nervous. Bobbito is a legend and I didn't want to do anything that would rub him the wrong way. When I showed up at the courts to introduce myself, he said, "How long are you going to take?"

At this moment, I knew he was the real deal. He was probably gauging to see if I was a cocky player who'd take my time, or if I'd take his workouts seriously.

I said, "Twenty seconds," as I tied my shoes, did a few stretches, and got onto the court.

The games were fast-paced with not many outside shots. Older guys were mixed in with younger guys and I made sure not to shoot too much. Even though the games were hard, it seemed like everybody knew each other and were very friendly.

Once we finished playing, Bobbito told me he liked my game and to come back again. I thanked him for letting me play, knowing I'd attend as many of these workouts as I could.

--

As time went on, working for the start-up got weird. There wasn't much work for me to do, as I'd send out hundreds of emails per day with a low response rate. Sometimes I'd bring a book and read while the other workers were in the front room figuring out strategy. After two months, my dad revealed that he had been investing money into the startup, which was basically paying my salary. I felt like a bum, since my dad was essentially paying for me to work there. I needed to find something else.

While looking for my next job, something happened that really shook me. One day, my grandma had a stroke and got hospitalized in New Jersey. Slurring her speech on the phone, she said, "Tyson, I'm going to die now. I love you, I love you…"

Frightened, I didn't know what to say, but knew I needed to go be with her.

I went to Camden, New Jersey, where she was being held in the ICU. For several days, my mom and I took turns sitting beside her hospital bed, feeding her ice chips and lending support. The whole time, I never heard my grandma complain. Only once she said, "It's funny. All I want is a simple glass of water but I can't even have that."

In the hospital, I did some deep thinking on what my future held. Taking a break for lunch one day, I walked over to a nearby cemetery. I looked at all the gravestones, wondering why I was still alive when all these other people had passed away already. It was a perplexing question, and it still is.

In the ICU with my mom, I bounced ideas off her. I told her I didn't want to just get a regular nine-to-five job yet, since I'd probably hate it. One thing I mentioned was how basketball had always provided me with direction. We questioned why I grew to be 6'6" tall, when the tallest person in our family was my grandfather, who was only about 6'3".

Keeping up the brainstorming, I gave Rick a call. I asked if there was any possibility I'd be able to play somewhere in the coming season. He mentioned an agent he knew in Argentina, adding, "But if you pull the shit you did in Sweden, they will kill you in Argentina. They will take you into an alley, beat the shit out of you, and leave you for dead. I promise you that."

Looking past the idea of getting left for dead in an alley somewhere, going to Argentina sounded interesting. It'd be a new part of the world, and nobody down there would have to know what happened in Sweden. I could just explain I was the leading scorer, the season ended, and I went back home. I knew I'd have to fit in with the team so I'd be sure to work on that.

With the possibility of Argentina, I felt a renewed sense of purpose. My grandma slowly got better and was eventually discharged from the hospital. I quit the start-up and started working as a grant writer for a healthy living company out of Philadelphia. I created a training program and started to get myself into shape. While people would finish work and go to Happy Hour at a bar, I considered my Happy Hour to be playing pickup basketball at the courts. At Bobbito's workouts I'd show up early and stay late, destroying everyone I played against. At the courts near my apartment, I started doing shooting and ball handling drills again. If anybody asked what my future held, I told them, "I'm going to play basketball in Argentina."

Knowing I needed higher-level competition if I wanted to thrive in South America, I called Coach Burden, my assistant coach from Maine. He told me about workouts at La Salle University in Philadelphia where Division 1 and pro guys played.

When I went to my first workouts there, I was in heaven. Every player there had played in college and most of them were on break between seasons overseas. I hadn't played against competition like this in a long time, and it felt great to battle again. I wasn't the best player, but I played my role, passing and shooting with the flow of the game. They got my defense tighter too, since they all played at high Division 1 schools.

This was the best run in the tristate area, so making a sacrifice was necessary. Two to three times per week, I took the 6:00 AM Chinatown bus to Philly so I could get to the gym on time. The grant writing job provided me the ability to work remotely, so I brought my laptop and worked on my way back to New York City. The commute wasn't ideal, but I knew if I wanted to be prepared for Argentina, this was what I had to do.

Discussing my plan with Rick again, he told me what would have to happen for a chance to play down there.

"Listen, Scooby Doo. First, you're going to have to pay for your own ticket down there. No team will pay for you to fly down, but if you're in the area, getting on a team will be a lot easier. Second, you'll need to try out for the teams, so you'll have to go to the different towns and make them like you. Once you get on a team, you can't mess it up. You have to stay the whole season, winning the championship if possible. Then we can get you on a better team the following year."

To me, all this sounded great. The risk was huge, but I was willing to do it for the possibility of a basketball career again. After playing with the high Division 1 guys in Philly all summer, I felt prepared for whatever competition would come my way.

As September approached, all signs pointed to Argentina. My sublet in Jersey City was coming to an end, the grant writing job out of Philly was dying down, and there were no other job prospects in mind. Every time I thought of Argentina, I got a surge of energy. I tried to learn Spanish and researched as much as I could about Argentinian culture.

I didn't know exactly how it would happen, but I felt that Argentina was the way.

--

Rick told me to fly into Cordoba, since he knew an agent there who could help me get on a team. Crowding over a laptop one night, my dad and I booked the one-way flight. It flew out of Miami and took about eight hours to get down there. My dad even helped me pay for it. It felt risky, but I trusted my skills.

As for where I'd stay when I got to Cordoba, I met a guy on CouchSurfing.com named Pablo who said he'd let me stay at his apartment for a few days. He spoke English, worked at a hospital, and looked eerily similar to Fefo. He also said he could pick me up from the airport, which was a huge plus.

Rick was wary about the guy from CouchSurfing, but there were no other alternatives. Hotels cost about $100 per night, which was too much for me at that time. I also wanted to be immersed in the local culture, not be some American living in a high-rise away from it all.

On the day of the flight, I called my family to say goodbye. I prayed that things would work out.

8
THE OTHER SIDE OF THE WORLD

The plane touched down in Cordoba, Argentina in the middle of the day in early September. Argentina is in the Southern Hemisphere, so September to March is their summer season. When I got off the plane, I immediately felt the heat.

Similar to the time in Sweden when I saw Oleg and immediately knew it was him, the same happened with Pablo. Intuitively seeing him, I said, "Pablo?"

Replying with an Argentinian accent, he said, "Yes…Tai-son?"

"Si, si, como estas??"

He laughed, "Oh, muy bien Espanol!"

"Gracias!"

I followed him outside, where we waited for the bus to his apartment in downtown Cordoba. I had no idea where I was so I was happy to have him as a guide. Pablo spoke perfect English so we chatted.

He inquired, "So you've never been down here before?"

"No, this is my first time."

"Okay, well you should be alright. Sometimes there's crime, but you're tall so nobody will mess with you. Do you like meat?"

"Yes, definitely."

"Ok, I'll cook an asado this week."

I had recently read about asado in a book about Argentinian culture and was excited to try it. It's an Argentinian barbeque with multiple kinds of meat.

When the bus came, we started the bumpy journey into the heart of Cordoba, which didn't look that much different from an American city. Curious, Pablo started asking me more in-depth questions. "So, what do you know about Argentina?"

From that simple statement, it was easy to see he had a lot of pride in his country. Extremely happy I did some research before I left so I didn't seem like an ignorant American, I replied, "Well, I know about the asados that you mentioned and I want to eat as much Argentinian food as possible. I know maté is the national drink, and there's a little ritual you perform while you enjoy it. Che Guevara was a country hero. Finally, Diego Maradona is the greatest soccer player Argentina's ever had, and I even read his autobiography."

Impressed by my knowledge, he replied, "Muy bien, Taison. You're not an ugly American."

We both laughed and I felt proud of myself for doing my research.

I did all that research because I wanted to fit in. Taking Rick's words seriously, I didn't want a repeat of Sweden. This could be my last chance to play professional basketball and I didn't want to mess it up. The plan was to make everybody love me so they wouldn't even think about kicking me off the team. Basketball would take care of itself. I knew I had the ability, I just needed the team to like me.

A young girl got on the bus with some books and sat in a seat directly in front of us. I looked at her and thought about how different our lives were. Here she was, going about her daily routine, probably heading home from school, while I just arrived from New York City hoping to get on a basketball team. But at the moment we were just two people on a bus heading to our final destination.

When our stop came, I felt the heat of the sun beating down on my head and thought, *Here we go... Argentina, baby.*

We walked down a dusty, winding road for about ten minutes, past Spanish-looking houses. Eventually we arrived in front of his apartment on the edge of a main street. The two-story building rested behind a large shopping mall.

Pablo's bachelor pad had a makeshift bed in the living room, a kitchen in the back, and a spiral staircase that led up to the second floor.

I said, "Me gusta su apartamento." (I like your apartment.)

"Gracias, Taison."

"De nada, hermano." (You're welcome, brother.)

I placed my bags on a chair as he arranged the pullout bed. He then gave me a tour. At the top of the spiral staircase was the entrance to his room. It was simple, with a full-sized bed on the left side and a dresser with a TV on the right. In the back corner was a door that opened out onto a patio.

Following him outside, he pointed to a grill and said, "We'll use that for the asado."

"Muy bien. I can't wait!"

When we went downstairs he said, "Do you need anything else, man?"

"No, eventually I want to get some food but I'm okay for now. Thank you so much, man."

He looked at me and replied, "You're welcome, but you need to start speaking Spanish. Necessitas aprender." (You need to learn.)

I was silent for a moment, doing the translation in my head, "Gracias por todos, hermano." (Thanks for everything, brother.)

He laughed, "Ok, good enough."

We gave each other a hug and he went back up to his room.

I thought, *Phew. So far, so good.*

--

I took a nap on the bed and when I woke up, I felt a surge of excitement about being in Argentina. I thought, *Not many people would do this: Buy a one-way ticket to Argentina to try out for different basketball teams, hoping to sign a contract without any guarantees.*

It was a major risk, but I told myself that no matter what, I was *not* going back home until I played on a team for the entire season. That was my only goal.

Opening up my Swedish laptop, I messaged a few family members. I didn't post anything to Facebook yet since I wanted to reserve that for when I actually got onto a team. Thinking about the agent Rick told me to contact, I looked through his Facebook friends for a guy named Ron. I couldn't find anybody with that name so I sent Rick a message.

While I waited for him to respond, Pablo came downstairs and asked if I wanted to get some food. Hungry from the trip across the equator, I followed him outside and to the supermarket across the street. Seeing authentic Argentina for the first time was exciting. The streets were dusty, motorcycles and mopeds lined the parking lot, and I was easily the tallest person in eyeshot. A few police officers stood guard nearby as stray dogs lied in the middle of the sidewalk.

Everything in the supermarket was in Spanish. A lot of the items were things I'd never seen before, so I stuck with the foods that I knew, like cereal and muffins. Honestly, I wanted to try all this new food but didn't want to spend all my money on the first day. I bought enough food for a few days then headed to the checkout counter.

I tried to use my debit card but it didn't work. The guy saw my Rowan ID and tried to use that, but I told him that definitely wouldn't work. Pablo paid with his own cash so we didn't hold up the line. Once we checked out, I found an ATM nearby and dispensed a few hundred pesos to pay Pablo back.

Back at the apartment, Pablo started cooking up some meat and I looked forward to my first Argentinian meal. For the next two hours, we discussed many topics: Basketball, girls, America, family, politics, Spanish, and life in general. He mixed in Spanish so I could start getting accustomed to the language. When we finished talking, he asked if I wanted to go to a dance club in the center of Cordoba. Not having any other plans, I agreed. We went out that night and danced to some Argentinian music, getting back home at around 4 AM.

The next day, Rick still hadn't gotten back to me about the name of the agent. I figured it was a long shot, but not knowing what else to do, I asked Pablo if he knew of an American basketball agent named Ron.

"Ron... no. I've never heard of him."

Thinking out loud, he continued, "However, I do know of a guy named Donald Jones. He was a star basketball player a few years ago for Atenas, the best team in Cordoba. Maybe that's him."

I looked up Donald Jones in Rick's contacts on Facebook. I found him and sent a message, explaining who I was. On his page he had lots of photos of basketball, so I hoped it was the right guy.

Waiting for a response, I explored Cordoba for a few hours by walking around the city. When I got back, Donald had messaged me with his phone number and email address.

I called from Pablo's house phone. It was the right guy, and he laid out the situation: I'd have to go to different towns to try out. If a team liked me, they'd sign me. If not, I'd have to go try a different one.

He explained, "The hardest thing about getting Americans on teams down here is that the teams don't know what they're getting. They can see a highlight tape, but it's expensive to fly these players down from America. The fact that you're in Cordoba already is huge because you won't cost the team any money for travel."

Getting more excited about my chances, I replied, "That's great man. I'm determined to get on a team."

"Okay well give me a few days to get in contact with some coaches. Message me your phone number so I can call you."

Not having a working cell phone yet, I replied, "Okay, I'll give you Pablo's house phone number."

"Who's Pablo?"

"Oh, he's the guy I'm staying with until I can get on a team. I met him through CouchSurfing."

"Okay. Oh yea, one more thing. There is a basketball tournament in Cordoba this coming weekend. I highly suggest you go so you can see what the competition is like out here. It's different than America."

"Ok, that sounds good. Where is it?"

"You wouldn't know. Is Pablo there? I can tell him the location."

"Yea, he's right here." I gave Pablo the phone and he talked to Donald for a few minutes in Spanish.

When they hung up, Pablo said to me, "Basketball tournament this weekend?!"

"Heck yea. You know where it is?"

"Yea, man. This is going to be fun."

Excited about the tournament and now having an American agent, it felt like things were starting to come together, which was a great sign. Now, I just needed to get on a team.

--

During the day, I took long walks through Cordoba. Nestled square in the middle of Argentina, it's the country's second-largest city and contains over a million people. Mapping out my path, I noticed a river and used it as my compass. Walking to the end of the river one day, I saw a large field where a few kids were playing soccer. The river bordered the field, with only a little hill preventing the ball from going into the water. The kids seemed to instinctively know how to prevent that from happening. I sat down next to a mother of one of the kids on the side and just watched for a while. I thought, *Once I make a lot of money over here, I'm going to pay for a huge net so these kids don't have to risk kicking the ball into the water.*

Across the street from the soccer field were hundreds of small shacks. I'd seen poverty in America, but nothing compared to this. With concrete walls and tin roofs, entire families lived in these small places. On the road in front of one of the houses, I saw some people crowded around a car. A guy was behind the driver's seat, smiling and honking the horn while everyone laughed. It looked like it was a new car and the family was driving it around for the first time. Even though they may not have had the biggest house in the world, they looked happy.

When the weekend came, Pablo and I went to the basketball tournament. We walked an hour through the hot sun to the gym, bringing our own food so we didn't have to pay for any at the concession stand. Arriving at the gym, it felt like I was back at home again. I saw the teams warming up, performing the same drills I'd done thousands of times throughout my life. In the stands were a few hundred people.

Atenas was playing, the most popular team in Cordoba and one of the best in the country. It was easy to see who the Americans were. There were three of them on the team and they were much bigger than the Argentinian guys. As the game started, I understood why Donald wanted me to come to this tournament. The style of play was different; scrappy, physical, and tough.

Players did things that looked like fouls but the refs didn't call them. On one play, a guy wrapped his arms completely around the opposing player, but the game continued. On another, gentle pushes to throw a player off balance would be called a foul in America, but here they played on.

During a break, Pablo said, "Hey man, you're trying to get on a team, right?"

"Yea."

"Okay, well there's the board of directors for Atenas right there. Go talk to them."

Shaking my head, I replied, "No, I barely speak Spanish. Plus, it doesn't work that way. They're not going to sign me to their team just because I walk up to them. I mean, what would I say, 'Hi, I'm Tyson from America, I want to play on your basketball team?'"

"No, but you could at least introduce yourself."

"I know, but Donald said he'd take care of it for me. I don't want to make a fool of myself."

"Okay, well if you won't, I'll go talk to them for you."

Pablo stood up and walked across the gym to the directors from Atenas, conversing with them for a few minutes. At one point they all looked over at me and I just smiled.

Pablo walked back over and handed me a piece of paper, "Ok, the person you need to talk to is Rico. Here's his phone number, and he said to call him tomorrow."

I looked at the paper and laughed, "What??!! You're awesome man!"

"This is Argentina… people are nice here."

The day after the tournament, I called Donald to see if he had any updates.

"Not yet man, but I'm working on it. Did you go see the games?"

"Yea, I went with Pablo. It was a good idea that I went, since I got to see how they played. Also, I got the number for a guy from Atenas who was at the game."

"Oh yea? What guy?"

"His name is Ricardo. He wants me to call him today."

He laughed, "I'm going to tell you this right now: Atenas already has their Americans for the season. Plus, they wouldn't sign you. This is your first year down here, so you have to establish yourself at a lower level then move your way up. That's how it works."

"Ok, so I shouldn't call him?"

Getting annoyed, he said, "Look, you can call him if you want, but remember what I just told you. I'm working for you, man."

Trusting and believing in him, I replied, "Okay, thanks for letting me know."

"No problem. Also, a bunch of us older guys are playing on Wednesday if you want to come up here and play. It's about a twenty minute taxi ride from where you are. Plus, I think it'll be good for you to get a run in."

Agreeing with him, I said, "Oh man that's perfect. I'll definitely be there, just message me the address."

"Okay, I will. Talk to you later."

I decided not to call Ricardo from Atenas since I trusted Donald.

Living at Pablo's apartment was perfect, but I couldn't stay there forever. He was going out of town for the weekend so I had to leave, but he said he'd help me get another place nearby. True to his word, a few hours later he told me of a friend who was renting rooms at a hostel down the street. I packed my bags and we headed down the main road in Cordoba.

Arriving at the front gate of the hostel, I was surprised to find that it was in a gorgeous house. The gate opened up to a small grassy yard, with shrubberies and a small garden. A young woman appeared in the doorway and gave Pablo a kiss on the cheek. I'd been in Argentina long enough to realize that everybody kissed on the cheek when meeting, whether it was two guys, two girls, or a guy and a girl. After saying hi, I greeted her with a kiss on the cheek as well.

We all entered the kitchen of the apartment as Pablo and Jane started speaking Spanish. After a few seconds, Pablo looked at me and said, "Quieres maté?" (Do you want maté?)

I replied, "Oh maté?? Si!"

They laughed at how excited I was as Jane prepared the maté. Maté wasn't just tea…it was a ritual.

It works like this: One person, the host, makes a thermos of boiling water. They put maté leaves into the bottom of a cup and pour the water over them. The host then drinks the maté through a bombilla, a metal straw. When the host is finished, they pour more hot water into the cup, passing it to the person next to them. He or she can then add sugar, but not water, since that's the job of the host.

Ideally, this ritual happens in the flow of conversation. If a person takes too long with drinking the maté, the host will tell them to hurry up. I'd never seen anything like it, and I was excited for my first experience with the process. When I finally took a sip, it tasted like a unique blend of thick herbal tea and sugar.

Performing the maté ritual, we discussed where I'd stay, how much the room would be, and for how long I'd be there. I picked up on some of the Spanish but was nowhere near fluent yet. Towards the end of the discussion, Jane showed me around the house.

We walked down two small steps to the living room, where two couches rested against the walls and there was a glass table in the center. In the corner of the living room was a door that opened to my room. Inside was a bed, closet, and dresser. I didn't know exactly how long I'd be there, but hoped it wasn't too long.

Pablo told me the rent was $200 per month with everything included. If I needed to move out, I should let them know a few weeks before so they could bring another person in. Excited about the price and the house, I agreed and Jane gave me the key.

I gave Pablo a kiss on the cheek before he left and thanked him for everything.

--

Pablo told Jane I was looking for a basketball team, so that night she mentioned a basketball gym nearby. I appreciated how much they were trying to help me.

When I got there the next day, nobody was in the gym but there was an older lady in the office. I tried to talk to her in what little Spanish I knew, "Hola, este el equipo de basquetbol?" (Hi, is this the basketball team?)

She blankly looked at me as I tried again, "Basquetbol team? Si? Hablas ingles?" (Basketball team? Yes? Speak English?)

She slightly understood what I meant, telling me she didn't speak English. However, she did write down a time on a piece of paper, explaining to come back then. I nodded and thanked her.

The writing on the paper said 19:00, but I arrived early at 6:30 PM. I didn't know what it was but figured I'd show up early anyway. I saw the same lady at the office and nobody was in the gym. Recognizing me from earlier, she left for a minute, then came back with a player.

In a deep Spanish accent, the player said, "Basquetbol?"

"Si."

He nodded and motioned for me to follow him. Entering the gym, I saw one set of creaky bleachers on the side. We walked across the court and into the locker room. I sat down next to him and he started to get changed into basketball clothes. Following his lead, I tried to spark conversation. "Hablas ingles?" (You speak English?)

He laughed, "Nooo, solamente Espanol." (No, only Spanish.)

"Oh, okay, mi espanol es mal." (Oh, okay, my Spanish is bad.)

Once changed, we went back out to the court, where more players started to show up. The player I was with started telling them about me in Spanish. I had no idea what they were saying but I hoped it was good. I didn't want to get beat up and left in an alleyway just yet, before I even had a chance to play on a team.

One of the guys named Mariano spoke up in perfect English, "You're here from America to play basketball?"

Hearing my native language was music to my ears. "Yes, I'm here to play on a team. I was told to come here and play with you guys."

"Okay, well I don't think we can pay you, but I'll ask the coach when he gets here."

Within minutes the coach showed up, an older Argentinian guy. He barely spoke English, but I introduced myself as Mariano explained my situation.

Mariano turned to me, "Okay, we'll figure out your situation later, but do you want to practice with us today?"

"Yes, definitely."

We started into it and it was just like anywhere else in the world. We warmed up, stretched, and did layups. When I started making nearly every shot, all the players, even the coaches, were impressed. To finish practice, we scrimmaged. The coach taught me some Argentinian words to say on defense. I proved that I was a great player, which felt great and very important.

After practice, Mariano took my number and told me to add him on Facebook. A few guys offered to drive me back to the apartment and, trying to fit in, I agreed. When we got in the car, they started driving the opposite way. I thought, *Oh shit, here we go. They're going to kill me and leave me for dead in an alleyway.*

Nervous about where we were going, I eventually spoke up. "Are we going the right way?"

In broken English they replied, "What's the address?"

"55 Calle."

The driver laughed, "Oh, I thought you said 155 Calles! Lo siento!"

He turned the car around as I breathed another sigh of relief.

Getting back to the apartment, I felt angry at myself for not knowing more Spanish. I had tried to learn it as much as I could before my trip, but I hadn't been very successful. If I didn't have Mariano speaking perfect English with me, I don't know what would have happened. I made a pact to myself to try to learn as much Spanish as I could, and to do it quickly.

--

Wednesday came and I was excited to play basketball again. It was another small gym with one set of bleachers. Donald wasn't there yet but there were some younger kids shooting. I put my bag down, picked up a ball, and started shooting, just like I'd done thousands of times in the past. A few minutes later Donald showed up with his teenaged son. Donald was from New Jersey, too, but had been living in Argentina for almost twenty years.

I approached Donald and said, "Nice to finally meet you."

"You as well. Have you been staying in shape?"

"Yes, as much as possible. I've been running along the river and played with Clubo Universario last night."

"Oh, you practiced with them?"

"Yea, they are right near where I live and said they might be able to get me on their team."

He rolled his eyes and said, "They won't be able to pay you at all. That's just a school team. I'm getting you a tryout next week, you've just got to stay in shape."

"Ok, awesome man, I will."

The older guys started to show up and we played five on five. I guarded Donald since he was still one of the better players and proved to him I had talent. I made shots, played great defense, and passed the ball well. After, he told me I had a nice shot but said I better be ready for the tryout. I thought, *Man, I've been preparing for this all summer.*

I stayed in shape over the next week by running along the river and lifting weights at a small gym nearby. There was nowhere to play basketball, but I trusted my skills wouldn't drop off too much in only a few days. A week from Wednesday, I got a call from Donald.

"Okay man, the tryout is tomorrow. The town is named Morteros and it's about two hours from Cordoba. You have to take the bus there."

"Holy crap! Thanks man! I've been training so I'm in good shape and ready for this."

"Ok, that's good. Don't bring all your stuff since it's only a tryout. I'll message you the coach's information and exactly where it is. Good luck man."

"Thanks so much Donald!"

I thought, *This is it! I'm finally getting my chance!*

The next day I went to the Cordoba bus station, which connects the entire country. Looking at the different destinations, I saw some busses went to Uruguay, others went to Chile, and others went to the southern tip of Argentina near Antarctica. Eventually, I found the window for Morteros and bought my ticket.

The bus was unlike anything I'd ever ridden on. It was a double-decker with an area on the bottom level for coffee, tea, or water. The seats reclined and were extremely comfortable. When the time of departure came, I laid back and relaxed.

Along the way, I appreciated the gorgeous landscape of Argentina. Cows lined the sides of the road and horses trotted off in the distance. It was a vast country that reminded me of the openness I saw when I drove from New Jersey to Chicago.

The bus pulled into Morteros two hours later. Unlike the huge station in Cordoba, Morteros only had two lanes for busses. On the inside there was only one row of benches. A short man in a basketball button-up shirt was sitting down. I sensed he was the coach just by the way he sat.

When I entered the station, he looked up and said, "Tyson?"

"Si."

"Hola, soy Jose, mucho gusto." (Hi, I'm Jose, nice to meet you.)

"Hola Jose, mucho gusto." (Hi Jose, nice to meet you.)

We spoke some English as he directed me to his tiny car. I put my bag in the back and got into the front seat. He said we'd go to the apartment to meet some teammates and then he'd drop me off at the hotel.

Opening my eyes to the scenery, Morteros was like paradise. Palm trees lined the road and behind them were two-story houses with impeccably clean driveways. We passed a park where a fountain spouted off water in the middle of a lake. I thought, *Damn, this place is gorgeous.*

After a short ride, Jose parked in front of a one-story apartment. He led me in through the garage. A few team members were watching TV. I introduced myself and noticed they were all over six feet tall.

After the introductions, Jose drove me to the hotel, where he said I'd stay for a night or two.

Before he left, he said, "Luis, the captain, will be over before practice to pick you up."

"Ok Jose, muchas gracias."

--

I had a few hours until practice later that day, so I got some food from downstairs then shaved to look presentable for the team. I knew I was ready but I still felt nervous. This was a huge opportunity and I needed to make the most of it. If I didn't make the team, I'd have to start all over again in a different town.

Almost finished shaving, I heard a knock. In the doorway stood a tall Argentinian with hair down to his shoulders.

He said, "Hola... Tai-son??"

"Si, eres Luis?" (Yes, you're Luis?)

"Si, como estas?" (Yes, how are you?)

We shook hands. He stood about 6'3" and I could tell he was a good player just by his physique.

I said, "Un momento," so I could finish shaving.

When I was ready, he said, "Oh, aca." I was bleeding a little bit from the shaving so he tore a piece of Kleenex from a box nearby and padded my face with it.

"Muchas gracias. Hablas ingles?" (Do you speak English?)

179

"Eh, mas o menos. Hablas espanol?" (Eh, more or less. Do you speak Spanish?)

"Eh, estoy tratando." (Eh, I'm trying.)

We smiled at the language barrier as I followed him out of the hotel and down to his small, two-door car. On the ride over, I got a better look at the town. It was secluded and rural, with one-story houses right next to each other. The streets were wide and dusty. I didn't see many restaurants or shops. The gym was on a secluded plot of land with a large soccer field in the back and a dirt track next to it.

Inside the gym was unlike any I had been in before. There was a balcony surrounding the court with bleachers on the sides. It had a rustic feel, with weight machines in the corner of the balcony and bird droppings on the court. I followed Luis to the locker room.

There were no physical lockers, just a small white room with a bench. The ceiling was at an angle so the further I went into the room, the more I had to duck. The guys were shouting in Spanish when I came in, and I had no idea what they were saying. We cheek-kissed and hugged like we'd known each other our entire lives. None of them spoke English, so I had to rely on the little Spanish I knew to introduce myself.

"Hola, soy Tyson."

They asked, "De donde vos?" (Where are you from?)

Not wanting to explain I was from a suburb in New Jersey about twenty minutes away from Philadelphia called Medford, I just said, "Nueva York."

Plus, I *had* technically lived in New York before, so it wasn't a lie.

We talked for a few minutes as we all got changed. As we shot around to warm up, I hoped I'd play well. I had confidence in my skills, now I just needed to prove them.

Practice started with a few drills until we got into the important part, the games. They played scrappy and physical so I adjusted to the style of play. I hit my shots, rebounded well, and played solid defense. I implemented a few things I learned from the team in Cordoba, like what to say on defense and how to react. Jose was impressed by my defense and taught me a few things he wanted me to say and do, like where to stand on offense and how to help out on defense. At the end I knew I played well, but I figured the next day would be the deciding practice on whether I would make the team.

Luis drove me back to the hotel and said he'd come by the next day at 5 PM to drive me to practice. In the room by myself, I lied down, praying this team would choose me. I didn't want to have to travel to a different city, since the season was going to be starting soon.

--

I woke up the following day, got some food, and prepared for practice. The sun was shining outside and the warm air felt amazing. On Facebook I saw a photo of Jersey City with a foot of snow, so I was happy to be in the warmth of Argentina.

At 5:00, Luis came by. On the court, I started to get used to the passionate effort of the players, realizing they weren't fouling, they were just playing hard. I matched their intensity, playing even harder but being cautious not to foul. Jose saw I could pass and liked my overall game. He praised me a few times and gave me instruction. I didn't overly dominate, but I felt I played well and performed when I got the ball. When practice finally ended, Jose motioned for me to follow him into the office, where two other team directors sat.

Sitting down, he said, "Okay Tyson, we are deciding to keep you on the team."

On the outside, I smiled and simply replied, "Ok, muy bien," but on the inside I thought, *Yes!! I did it!!*

Over the next few minutes, we worked out an agreement for how long I'd be on the team, how much they'd pay me, and where I'd live. They were speaking Spanish so I only understood a few words here and there. I was fine with that though, because the details didn't matter. I was on a team. I signed some papers and they told me when I should come back to town. I gave them all hugs and walked back into the gym.

When I got back to the locker room, the players were all changing.

Luis said, "Si?"

Pausing for dramatic effect, I replied, "Si. Estoy en el equipo!" (Yes. I am on the team!)

The entire team immediately started cheering and congratulating me. I was only in Morteros two days, but I loved it already.

--

I traveled back to Cordoba the following day to get the rest of my belongings. When I got back, I told Pablo and Jane that I got on a team and they were both happy for me. I told Jane I'd have to give up the apartment and she gave me the bill. For my two-week stay in a nice room with all utilities paid for, I only had to pay $100. I thought, *Argentina, baby.*

I messaged everybody back home the good news. I was only going to be paid about $1,000 a month, but the team was going to pay for food and housing. Donald didn't tell me I owed him a commission so I figured the team would pay him.

At this point I felt extremely proud of myself. Buying a one-way plane ticket to another country to try out for teams had been a huge risk. Coupled with the fact that I didn't know anybody, didn't have the right name of the agent, and didn't speak much Spanish, I was truly happy. Things could have easily not worked out, but I owed it all to the preparation I put in over the summer.

Arriving back at the bus station in Morteros, Jose wasn't waiting for me. In fact, nobody was. I didn't have a working cell phone so I just looked around, pondering what I should do next. After a few minutes, I decided the best plan was to walk in the general direction of the house that Jose brought me to on the first day. I didn't know exactly where it was, but hoped I'd remember as I started walking.

Throwing my bags across my back, I started the walk in the hot Argentinian sun. After a while a guy pulled up next to me on his moped. He was one of the staff members I saw the day before and had a big smile on his face.

He said, "Hola Taison! A donde vos?" (Where are you going?)

"La casa, pero yo no se donde exactamente." (The house, but I don't know exactly where it is.)

He motioned for me to get on the moped. I put my bag on the back. It seemed dangerous but I had no other options. We picked up speed, and he started shaking the front wheel back and forth. I felt for certain we were going to crash, but we finally straightened out. After a short ride he stopped in front of the house Jose had brought me to on the first day.

He waved goodbye and sped off. I walked through the garage, just as Jose had done, and opened the door to the kitchen. At the table Luis sat with another teammate.

We hugged and cheek-kissed. Luis showed me to my room down the hall, where I put my bags on the floor. It was spacious and had a queen-sized bed and large dresser in the corner. Sunlight shone in from two windows at the head of the bed.

Luis said in broken English, "You room."

"Muchas gracias hermano."

He pointed to his stomach, "Eat?"

"Si, si, por favor."

"Muy bien, veni..." (Very good, come...)

In the kitchen, a large plate of food waited for me. I tried to talk to them over food, but the language barrier was too difficult. I spoke a little Spanish but not enough to have a decent conversation.

I got an idea and said, "Tienes internet?"

Luis said, "Si." I brought out my laptop, put in the internet code and went to Google Translate.

I typed in sentences, translated them to Spanish, then showed them the computer screen. It started to work and they understood what I said.

When they had something to tell me, they did the same thing, then translated it to English. I was happy we were communicating, one Google Translate sentence at a time.

The hour of practice came and it felt amazing being an official member of the team. Getting more accustomed to the style of play, I played more physical than I had been used to. The coaches loved this so I kept it up. Even though I was officially on the team, I needed to keep proving myself every day.

After practice, all the teammates hung out at our house. It reminded me of college, only everybody spoke Spanish. Through Google Translate, I told them about where I was from, what life was like in America, and where I played basketball before. They seemed to like me, which was my number one goal since I didn't want a repeat of Sweden.

--

A Day in the Life

The sun's rays beam into the window above my bed, waking me up. I open my eyes and feel the warmth of the Argentinian summer, my body already starting to perspire. As I slide out of bed I feel the warm tiles beneath my feet. I think, *Here I am, deep in Argentina, playing professional basketball.*

After a few seconds of happiness and gratitude, I walk to the kitchen. Luis is already off to work at a cell phone repair shop and Juan, my other roommate, is still sleeping in the room next to mine. I open the cabinet, removing the biscuits and instant coffee. Since I'm going to the gym soon, I'm having a light breakfast, with a real meal coming after the workout.

While heating up the water, I step out onto the outdoor patio. It's a cement enclosure with a sturdy table in the middle and a grill on the side for asados. I close my eyes and look up at the sun, basking in the rays permeating my skin.

I head back inside, pour the coffee, and eat a few biscuits while seeing what's happening in the world on my laptop. Same stuff, different day.

Finishing the biscuits in my room, I get changed for the workout.

Typically, we'll have one practice per day with optional shooting or weight lifting in the morning. Sometimes we'll have two mandatory practices per day. Today I'm going to shoot with a few guys and maybe lift some weights before it gets too hot in the gym.

After putting on my shoes, I stick my headphones in my ears and turn on a new mix by Tiesto or Armin van Buuren. I start my fifteen-minute trek to the gym. Along the way I see people cleaning their driveways and living what appear to be quiet lives. This isn't New York City, where people are wheeling and dealing, trying to make as much money as possible. These people take care of their property and family but money seems less important than it is in America.

Nearing the gym, I see an older man who sits on his chair with his cane in a propped position. He's out there every day, just watching the cars and people go by, observing it all. For all I know, he could have been doing this for the past twenty years. In that moment, I hope I can provide him with some excitement, being a 6'6" guy from America.

Arriving at the gym, I see the clothing manager, Choche. He doesn't speak English but I still laugh at whatever he says. His job is to make sure all the uniforms are clean and the court is washed. We give each other a kiss on the cheek, then I head into the locker room to get changed.

In my gear, I walk upstairs to the balcony where the weights are. There are only a few dusty machines with light free weights. To me, it seems dangerous since the bars seem too small. I think, *Okay, once I make a lot of money here I'm going to buy new weights.*

I go through a chest and triceps workout, finishing with ab exercises. A few other guys start to show up down below so I walk down the staircase to the court. I especially like these teammates because they work hard. Here, it's natural to wake up and shoot three hundred shots, eat, then practice later in the day. Growing up with the same work ethic, I fit right in.

We start the shooting drills as a few stray dogs run across the gym. There's a spot at center court with bird droppings from a nest above. We pay these obstacles no mind as we continue the workout, which includes shots, moves, and sometimes sprints. At the end, we shoot free throws, followed by stretching. A few of the guys head to the pool behind the gym, but I'm hungry so I get changed and leave.

Morteros isn't like a typical city, where you can go to a deli or restaurant and get whatever food you want. The team provides us with a certain place to eat lunch and dinner every day. Similar to the restaurant in Sweden, I tell them if I want chicken or fish, then they wrap up a plate of food and hand it to me. The food is good, but if I want something else I don't have a choice. I either eat what they give me or I go hungry.

At the house, I eat then do my laundry. That chore is a little different than what I was used to. The washing machine is in an enclosed area on the patio. The machine is actually just a big barrel that moves the clothes around. I fill it with water from a hose, add my clothes and the detergent, then plug it in. The machine will go on indefinitely if I don't pay attention, so I set my alarm for thirty minutes.

When the clothes are washed, I drain the water. There is no dryer, so we must pin our clothes on the line stretching from opposite sides of the patio. Feeling how people must have felt without electricity, I pin the wet clothes on the line. The sun will ruin the material if they stay out too long, so I set the alarm once again.

Once I fold the dry clothes, there are still a few more hours until practice. In mid-day right after lunch, the entire town of Morteros shuts down for siesta, a rest period many Spanish countries take during the hottest part of the day. Here, the town shuts down from 1 PM to 5 PM. No businesses are open and nobody is on the streets. I'd heard of a siesta before, but never knew how seriously they took it. I laugh at the idea of New York City shutting down for four hours in the middle of the day.

I'm not tired so I go to a teammate's house down the street. I help him with English as he helps me with Spanish. Then we play the video game FIFA Soccer.

In the United States, I knew some guys who played the video game, but in Argentina, everybody plays and is amazing at it. Maybe it's because they grew up playing soccer or maybe they just play a lot, but I never beat any of them. This pissed me off and I tried to practice when nobody was around, but I still never won.

After the video games, I go to one of my favorite places in Morteros, the ice cream shop. It's the only place that's open during siesta. The lady behind the counter says, "Hola flaco, que necesitas?" (Hey skinny, what do you need?)

I take mild offense to that, since I work out all the time and don't think of myself as skinny. However, I learn that "flaco" is a nickname that Argentinians use for anybody who's in shape.

"Dulce de leche, por favor."

She scoops me a cup of the epic ice cream and I pour some syrup over it. I pay with my pesos then walk out into the hot Argentinian air.

When practice comes, I walk the same route to the gym I used earlier in the day. Getting to the locker room, I cheek-kiss the guys while saying the new Spanish word "Boludo." It's an Argentinian word that has many meanings, and they all laugh when I use it.

Practice is similar to the day before as we run plays and scrimmage. I hold my own, making sure the bigger guys don't push me around. Sometimes they get dirty, so I get dirty back. If I get an elbow, I'll throw one back. Not in a malicious way, but just to let them know I'm there. If I give an inch, they'll take five inches and I can't let that happen. When practice is over, we all clean up by going into the showers.

My first time in the showers with these guys was an experience. I've obviously showered with guys before, but here, they were completely open with each other… maybe too open. I sit on the bench and take my clothes off, waiting for an open spot. Meanwhile, they all shout and walk around each other, staring at each other's naked bodies. I think, *Okay, I hope I can just find a shower head and clean up without them noticing me.*

Waiting for a shower, my teammate who I played FIFA with earlier says, "Hey Tyson, check out Tomas. He has a huge penis."

Laughing while averting my eyes, I reply, "That's great man."

He pushes the issue, "No, seriously man, check it out. It's huge."

Smiling again, I say, "No man, I'm okay."

He taps my shoulder and says again, "Look man, you gotta check it out!"

Giving in, I look up at Tomas directly across from me. He's sitting there completely naked with a grin of self-pride as I notice what my teammate wants me to look at. I shake my head and start laughing.

I spot an open shower in the back and walk towards it. On my way there, a few of the guys look at me, checking out my naked body. In front of the shower head, I start to wash while covering up, since I can feel the stares from my teammates.

After a few seconds, my roommate Juan approaches me. He screams, "Tai-son, mira!"

When I look over, Juan is tucking his penis between his legs and rubbing his nipples, pretending like he's a woman.

He prances around the showers saying in a high-pitched tone, "Estoy una mujer! Estoy una mujer!" (I'm a woman!)

Everybody laughs. He turns to me and says, "You be a woman! You be a woman!"

I think, *Shit, I want to fit in, but I'm not going to prance around the showers acting like a woman.*

I smile and say, "No, estoy bien. Estoy bien." (I'm good.)

He keeps egging me on, but I keep saying no. Eventually, he lets it rest and dries off. The other teammates dry off as well and head home for the night. I'm left in the shower by myself, thinking about the craziness that just occurred. I finish, change into dry clothes, and make my way back to the house.

Juan and Luis are eating at the kitchen table when I arrive. We talk a little bit, using Google Translate to fill in the missing words. I eat my tray of food with them, then relax in my room for the rest of the night. Here, I

Skype family members or read.

Eventually I go to sleep, knowing that tomorrow will be extremely similar.

--

On days that I didn't play FIFA with my teammates, I sat next to the lake by the library and wrote. I'd write short stories or letters to family and friends back home. The library, I found out, didn't have any English books, so I was forced to read books on my laptop. My mom tried to send me a Kindle but it got lost or stolen in the mail. Sitting by the fountain on these warm days with palm trees lining the road, it felt romantic as I wrote, getting lost in a story that took me away from Morteros for a few hours.

As for basketball, the reason I was there, when games started I became one of the leading scorers. I started every game and averaged nearly 15 points per game with 8 rebounds. Whether the game was home or away, I played my role, doing what was necessary for the team. After a few games we had a winning record and things were looking up.

One night after practice, Jose came to the house and told me he needed me to be more aggressive on the court. I nodded my head, agreeing I would make it happen. I agreed, but knew I couldn't be too aggressive. This was basketball, not football. If a player is too aggressive then they play out of control. There is a fine line between aggression and control, and I balanced the line.

As two months went by, we were winning and I was scoring, but I felt homesick again. In the entire town, it seemed like few people spoke English, which made communication difficult. My Spanish was coming along, but not nearly enough to have a fluid conversation with anybody.

In the warmups of a home game one night, I thought about how different my life was compared to other people from college. I thought, *Here I am…Saturday night in this small town deep in the middle of Argentina. I'm nervous about this game because I have to keep scoring points and winning games, while the only worry my friends probably have is what beer to drink tonight.* I wished there was another American in the town to talk with.

A week later, my wish came true. A player arrived from America who was from New Jersey. He wasn't on our team; he was on the other team in Morteros. Regardless, I was happy to have him in town. We talked a few times and although we didn't become best friends, it was great to get his perspective on it all. He'd been playing overseas for a while so he knew what it was like.

When December came, our record was solid. The road trips exposed me to more of the gorgeous Argentina countryside, which I loved. On one road game, we played against an American on the opposing team. Afterwards, I went up and talked to him, since every American at this point was like a gift. He said he was from Camden, New Jersey, and he even knew of one of my ex-teammates from Rowan. I thought, *This is so cool. We're both deep in Argentina and know the same player from Camden.* I got his contact information and we stayed in touch.

After games, both teams typically ate together. The host team would grill up some sausages and put them in a roll, distributing them to the players. Coca-Cola was also a huge staple of the culture, as players drank it before and after games.

Similar to Sweden, I was playing in the lowest league of the country. Only a few hundred people attended these games, mostly fans from the town or family members of the players. The crowds sometimes got rowdy though, which I loved.

Halftime of a home game provided me a true glimpse of Argentinian culture. All packed into our locker room to listen to our coach Jose, one jug of water started at the end of the wraparound bench. The first player drank out of it then passed it to the next player. That player drank it then passed it to the next. The jug went around the room until I was the last one in line. There was only a small amount left, most likely all backwash. Hoping nobody was watching, I just set the jug on the ground. I wanted to fit in and make them like me, but there were some things I was not willing to do.

Another thing I noticed was that Morteros had a huge fireworks store. Why this little town needed heavy-artillery fireworks, I had no idea. But I loved fireworks so I bought some one day. I didn't buy the big ones, just the little M-80's that make a loud bang when you light them. As long as you don't light it near a body part, they're harmless.

One day when Luis was mowing the grass outside, I thought I would mess with him. I lit an M-80 and threw it near the lawn mower. It wasn't too close, but close enough for him to hear it. When it exploded, I saw him jump up and turn around. When he looked at me, he smiled with a look that said, "Ok Tai-son, I'll get you back..."

A few days later, I groggily woke up and went into the kitchen for breakfast. I lazily ate my food as Juan and Luis were finishing up. As I was eating, Juan stood up and started laughing, walking away from the table. I wondered what he was laughing at when I looked to my right and saw a lit M-80 right next to my food. I thought, *Fuck!*

Seconds later, it exploded right next to my face. I dropped my fork and ran out of the house, feeling the blood pumping to my ears. I couldn't hear anything for over a minute, which was terrifying. When my hearing returned, I went back into the house and saw Juan and Luis laughing at me. Thinking this wasn't funny, I put some clothes into my bag and walked over to the gym to shoot. I was pissed off because that M-80 could have really done some damage. Not wanting to take my rage out on them, I took it out on the court.

Later at practice, one of my teammates asked me what happened. I replied, "Luis es un boludo," which in context means "Luis is an idiot." The teammate walked to Luis and told him, and they all started laughing. I was still mad but smiled anyway.

--

Our team wasn't playing any games from Christmas to New Years, so I wanted to set up a trip to see more of Argentina. A ticket back to America was too expensive, so I researched where I could go to get out of Morteros for a while. In my research, everybody talked about Mar Del Plata, a beachside town on the east coast of the country. Looking into it, I thought that would be a perfect place to spend my Christmas. I booked a hotel and got excited for the trip.

In the last game before Christmas break, I felt an extreme sense of pride. I took a huge risk by flying down to Argentina without being on a team.

Now, here I was, ten games in as the leading scorer with a solid record. From what I gathered, everybody on the team liked me, because I liked them.

During halftime of the final game, Jose brought the team outside to discuss the plan for the second half. I was feeling great since I had about 15 points in the half and we were winning by 10. When he started talking, I realized that I understood everything he was saying. Typically I would only understand single words, but never full sentences. My pride swelled even further, happy with the fact I was starting to learn this language. Getting back onto the court, I felt even better than before and we won the game handily.

Outside under the stars after the game, we ate with the opposing team. Everybody was feeling jolly since we were going on a break for a while and got to relax. A bottle of champagne was passed around and I took a few sips.

When we all had our fill of hydration and food, Jose motioned for me to follow him into the gym. I walked behind him and our assistant coach joined us. I wasn't worried at all, knowing that the team liked me, I was playing well, and we were winning games. I wondered what he wanted to talk about. I hoped it was about an increase in pay or that we'd be bringing in another American. Both of these ideas got me excited.

In the locker room, Jose started speaking in broken English, "Taison, we really like you. You are a great player and a great teammate."

"Gracias Jose."

"Unfortunately though, we are going to have to bring in a different American."

I thought, *Nooo, nooo, nooo, this can't be happening. Noooooo.*

Trying to clarify what he meant, I asked, "What do you mean, there will be two Americans?"

"No, there's only one. You won't be on this team anymore because we're bringing in someone else."

It was happening. My worst nightmare…again. Not having any clue this was coming, but being a professional, I asked, "Por que?" (Why?)

He replied, "Necessitamos un jugar mas alto quien puede salta mas." (We want a player who's taller and who can jump higher.)

I thought, *Are you kidding me?! I'm the tallest player on this team and one of the highest jumpers.*

Having been through this before, I asked them a few questions. "Pero, tengo el mejor puntos y rebotes en el equipo. Por qué?" (But I have the most points and rebounds on the team. Why?)

"Los directores quieren un nuevo jugador. Lo siento Taison." (The directors decided they want a new player. I'm sorry Tyson.)

It wasn't his choice but that still didn't change the situation. Basketball was a business and I was a tool. That was it. There was nothing I could do about it so I stopped fighting and accepted it.

Trying a final time, I asked, "Entonces, hay nada yo puedo hacer? Este definamente?" (So there's nothing I can do? This is definitive?)

"Si Tyson, lo siento. You can stay in the town until New Years, but once practices start up, you're going to have to leave."

Resigned to my fate, I said, "Okay, gracias."

We shook hands and walked outside to where my teammates were laughing and drinking champagne. I sat back in my chair and thought, *What the fuck.*

9
"YOUR DREAMS JUST CAME TRUE"

I was shocked by what happened but I was a professional. There was nothing I could do so there was no reason to get upset about it. The part that hurt was how hard I worked to fit in and be a great teammate. I even grew my hair long to try to fit in more.

At this point I knew basketball was a business, but it still sucked. Unlike a regular job, there was no severance pay, benefits, or pension plan. Maybe they could help me get on another team, but it seemed unlikely. When they said get out, I had to get out. End of discussion. I didn't know how I would tell my dad and Rick, since they'd just tell me my basketball career was definitely over.

Not losing all hope, I messaged Donald to see if I could get onto a different team. He told me it was possible and he'd ask around. While I waited for him to come back with an answer, all I wanted to do was relax at the beach in Mar Del Plata. I thought some down time would help me figure out my next steps.

I had to get out of Morteros before practices started in January, but until then I left some of my belongings in the room. Bringing all my valuables, I got on the bus. After a stop in Buenos Aires, the final leg took me down the coast. The hotel rested at the edge of the beach, while the bus station resided in the center of the city. I estimated it would take about thirty minutes to walk to the hotel so I put my bag over my back and started the trek.

The city was gorgeous, even more beautiful than the photos online. Shops, bookstores, and restaurants lined the main road while palm trees lined the sidewalks. Stopping at a bookstore in the middle of my journey, I was elated to find a huge section of English books. I bought a few for

Christmas, vowing to return and pick up some more before I left this paradise for good.

I continued the walk down the main street until the road opened up to the ocean. Approaching the edge of the sea, more beauty filled my eyes. The beach stretched on for miles, with a boardwalk lining the sand, where people could buy beach supplies or snacks. Happy I chose this city for Christmas, I soaked up the sights.

When I checked in I got a room on the second floor. It was small, with one full-sized bed and a small bathroom. Completely okay with this, I dropped my bags onto the floor and lay down on the bed. After a few minutes I put on my sandals and walked down to the beach.

At water's edge, I put my feet into the surf and looked out at the ocean. I thought about my situation, but kept telling myself there was nothing else I could do. I thought, *Might as well just enjoy Mar Del Plata.* I had no regrets and did everything I could for the team to keep me, but I couldn't control the desires of the directors. God had gotten me this far and I was happy with that. I was hoping Donald could get me onto a different team for the remainder of the season, but for the time being, I relaxed.

--

I was nervous spending Christmas alone because I thought I'd feel sad and depressed, but when the day finally came I felt great. The NBA started playing again after the lockout, so I was excited to watch Kobe play Lebron. After getting a long sleep, I went to the local restaurant to watch the game. In Spanish, I asked the waitress if she could turn on the NBA. She asked if I meant the soccer tournament, but I pointed her to the NBA listing. She scrolled down, pressed the button, and a basketball court appeared on the screen. By the beach, on Christmas day, eating Argentinian food, watching the Heat play the Lakers, I was in heaven.

Since this was Argentina, nobody cared much about the NBA. When great plays happened, I screamed, "Ohhhh," while couples next to me wondered what the hell my problem was. After the game, I Skyped my family and wished them all a Merry Christmas. To finish off the day, I walked up and down the coast of Mar Del Plata observing the sights and sounds of the area. At the end of the walk, I deduced that we human beings are all extremely similar, whether we live in New Jersey or Mar Del Plata. We want the same things, just the locations are changed.

At one of the shops where I bought snacks, I met a cute Argentinian girl. She couldn't talk long because she was working. When I looked to the back of the store, her parents behind the counter were staring daggers at me. She was very pretty so she probably got approached all the time. If I lived in that town I would have tried to take her out, but I was only there for a day so it would have been useless.

The day after Christmas, Mar Del Plata got crowded. Hordes of people filled the streets and beaches, their Christmas Day celebrations over with. Since this was one of the best beaches in Argentina, families arrived from thousands of miles away to go there, just like I had done. Fortunately for me, I was leaving on the 26th anyway, heading back to a city that didn't even want me.

On the day of my departure, I packed my bags, kissed the beach goodbye, and trekked to the bus station, stopping at the bookstore along the way to pick up a few more English books.

I had a few more days until New Year's so I planned to stay in Buenos Aires for a day, since I had no reason to be in Morteros. I thought it'd be great to check out this famous city. When I got there my first goal was to find a coffee shop with internet access. I didn't have a smartphone, so I couldn't use GPS. I wandered the city for a few hours, trying to find a place where I could go online and book an inexpensive hotel for the night. Getting frustrated, I eventually noticed the logo up in the distance: Starbucks.

Was it a mirage? I hoped not.

Getting closer, I'd never been so happy to see a Starbucks in my life. I paid five dollars for a drink and plopped my tired body down on a cushioned chair overlooking a river. Opening up my laptop, I connected to the internet and researched hotels in the area. Finding a fancy yet inexpensive one right down the street, I called to make sure they were legit. They spoke English, which was another plus. I booked the room and headed over.

The hotel wasn't in the best neighborhood, but when I opened the doors it felt like I was in another world. Blue lights, soft music, and a receptionist who spoke perfect English greeted me. My room was even classier, with a queen-sized bed, a desk, a walk-in shower, and a balcony that opened up to the genuine sounds of Buenos Aires. I felt like a king, if only for a night.

Connecting to the internet, I Skyped my mom and sent a few emails. Then I walked around the city for a while. Following a sidewalk along a park, the Argentine romanticism hit me.

The lights, the trees and the warm air, were like nothing I'd ever experienced. I wished I had a girl with me at that moment, but I was still happy to be there. I bought delicious meat on a bun from a stand then made my way back to the hotel. The bar had filled up but I went straight up to my room, where I pulled out a book and read myself to sleep.

When the sun woke me up, the realization hit me that I had to go back to Morteros. Passing the lobby on the way out, I saw there was a pool. Hoping to see some girls lounging, I instead saw all guys in tight bathing suits. In the lobby, I noticed some pamphlets for gay bars in the area. I realized then that I had stayed at an LGBT (Lesbian, Gay, Bisexual, Transsexual) hotel. I didn't even know there was such a thing, but damn it was classy.

Lugging my bag to the bus station, I stopped at a pizza place before the trip. Next to the bus station was an impoverished area, and when I sat down I sensed people staring at my stuff, as if wondering if I would leave it out of sight for just an instant. An hour later, I got on the bus back to Morteros, hoping that Donald would come through with another team to try out for.

--

Once I got there, I went to the track behind the gym to do some sprints, to keep my mind occupied. But by the end of the workout, I was mad at myself. Once again, I had gotten kicked off a team and kicked out of a town. I thought, *Really, God? Really? You're just messing with me now, right?*

I took some solace in the fact that I had done everything I could to stay on this team, on and off the court. I hoped there was something better in store but bouncing around from team to team was taking a toll mentally and emotionally, and I questioned if I even wanted to play basketball anymore.

After my workout I ran into Tuti, a 37-year-old teammate who was still talented. I broke the news that I was leaving and a look of sadness washed over his face. Still, he'd been playing for a long time and knew basketball was a business. We gave each other a hug then went our separate ways.

I was going to miss everybody. They were the most genuine, warm people I'd ever met in my life. From the first day in the town, everybody treated me like I had been a part of the community for years. I'd never felt this way before. Morteros gave me a new perspective on life and gave me hope for civilization.

New Year's came and I celebrated with Luis and his family. When the clock struck zero, it seemed like Morteros was a warzone, with all the mortars and fireworks lighting up the sky. It was beautiful, but I was sad to be leaving the town. My Spanish had gotten better, so I was able to talk to Luis and his family as we ate our final asado together.

I overheard him tell his girlfriend in Spanish, not knowing I could now understand him, "El quiere escribir mucho." (He likes to write a lot.) I hadn't known he noticed me writing.

On January 1st, Donald messaged me on Facebook. He said, "Hey man, I haven't got anything for you. Maybe you should think about going home. It's kind of hard now. Everybody wants big guys."

I replied, "Ok, well are there different countries I could play in, or other cities?"

"I don't know man. Most teams are on their vacation now. And since a provincial team didn't want you, it's going to be impossible to get you on a higher team. What are you going to do now?"

"Since I can't stay in Morteros, I'm going back to Cordoba for the time being. If anything pops up, let me know. I'll stay in shape just in case."

"Okay man, I'll keep looking for you."

At that point, I resigned to the fact I wasn't going to get on a different team. My dad was coming down to Chile in February for vacation, so if I didn't get on a team, the goal was to just meet him there and fly back to the states with him. But that was still over a month away and I didn't know what I would do until then.

On New Year's Day, Luis helped me bring my stuff to the small Morteros bus station. Almost crying, I gave him a big hug and said, "Gracias por todos hermano, en serio." (Thank you for everything man. Seriously.)

"Che… No hay problema." (Ey… no problem.)

"Che… Eres un boludo."

He laughed, "Eres un boludo grande."

I laughed with him and said, "Te amo hermano, hablamos en Facebook." (I love you man, let's talk on Facebook.)

"Si, yo lo escribe en facebook." (Yes, message me on Facebook.)

We gave each other a final hug and kiss on the cheek, and I stepped onto the bus. I sat down and watched him drive off in his car.

--

I stayed at Pablo's place in Cordoba, my only hope being that Donald would come through. I didn't want to go home yet, since my goal remained to finish out a full season. Obviously it would no longer be with the same team, but I could still finish out the season somewhere. To stay in shape, I worked out along the river and went to a gym. Some days I walked through the city of Cordoba all day long.

Several days went by and things were looking bleak. I ate with Pablo and did what I could to not worry about my situation too much. All the while, I stayed prepared just in case.

On January 8th, 2012, I got a message from Donald on Facebook. For some reason, he was using all caps, "I MIGHT HAVE SOMETHING FOR YOU IN CHILE. ARE YOU INTERESTED. SEND ME A MESSAGE… YOU ARE PROBABLY LEAVING TUESDAY OR

WEDNESDAY."

Another message followed, "I GOT YOU A JOB IN VALDIVIA, CHILE."

When I got these messages, I was elated. I thought, *I knew there was a reason I stayed down here. I felt it.*

I messaged Donald immediately and he emailed me the details. It was a two-week contract and if we won, we'd play in the playoffs. The team would pay for everything, even a flight back to the states once the season finished. I appreciated that because although I liked South America I knew I couldn't stay there forever.

Pablo was at work on the day of my departure and I wanted to thank him somehow, so I wrote him a note, cleaned his bathroom, and left him an English book I thought he'd like. His friend Maria, who I actually talked to through Skype once in Morteros, came by to pick up my key. I could tell we were both interested in each other but the language barrier was tough. When I told her I was leaving for Chile a sad look crossed her face. I would have liked to get to know her better but basketball was the pressing issue at the time. I gave her a hug, handed her the key to Pablo's apartment, then got in a taxi to the Cordoba airport.

Since I was in Argentina over three months, I had to pay the country 350 pesos. Fortunately I had some cash on me, otherwise there may have been a problem. I got through security and went to the gate, heading to Santiago, Chile. The coach was going to pick me up when I got there and drive us down to Valdivia, the city where the team was based.

Waiting for the plane, I saw a bunch of Americans who were on a hunting trip. I desperately wanted to talk to them in English, but I thought it would be weird. So I minded my own business. As I waited, a sign from God appeared to me loud and clear.

In the line to board the plane, I noticed that a young Spanish girl had a shirt that read, *Your dreams just came true.*

It was a simple, cliché shirt, but I laughed. I thought, *Really? Was this my dream? Was playing on my third team in three countries in two seasons my dream? Or was it the best I could do?* Then I wondered, *Were the experiences worth more than the wins and losses?*

In Santiago, I found the coach, who spoke decent English. We discussed a few things on the way, like where I'd be living, who I'd be staying with, and when practices were. He said the important thing was that we win games, since we were close to the playoffs.

At the apartment in Valdivia, he introduced me to my roommate. He was an American from Virginia. I was happy that we could have a real conversation about everything that went on. He was even bigger than me, 6'8", and had been playing professional basketball all across the world for the past seven seasons.

We practiced the next day at a small gym nearby, where I met the team for the first time. The players weren't that great and I was one of the most talented, even though I wasn't in perfect basketball shape. The game was on the weekend, so we had a few days of practice to get accustomed to each other. Practices weren't that hard since it was nearing the end of the season.

Walking home from practice one warm evening, I was wearing my jersey, with my bag slung across my back. I dribbled a basketball down the sidewalk past a few houses. A bus let off some people, a few of them workers coming home from their jobs. One guy, a Chilean man about my age in a suit and with a briefcase, walked in my direction.

In that moment, I realized how unusual my life was. While someone my age would typically be dressing up in nice clothes and working a nine to five, here I was in a jersey, coming home from my job playing basketball in South America. I smiled at this, knowing it was exactly what I always wanted to do. To me, it felt right.

The city of Valdivia seemed fairly Americanized. A McDonald's sat in the center of town and a few people spoke English. It was also a tourist destination, so there were attractions like fishing, hiking, and boat tours. There was a fish market at the edge of town, with manatees hanging around waiting for the leftovers. Our apartment complex rested on the edge of the lake, overlooking a forested mountain. Similar to Argentina and Sweden, we were provided lunch every day at a restaurant.

Our first game was on a Saturday about an hour away. The gym had a coliseum-style feel to it, with bleachers surrounding the entire court. The team we played was one of the best in the league and had a great record, so fans packed the gym. When we started the game, I felt off, like something was wrong.

As the game progressed, I realized the reason I felt that was because the style of play was completely different than in Argentina. There, it was scrappy and hard-nosed, with lots of grabbing and near-fouls. In Chile, it was American basketball with less defense. The teams played solid defense, but not the high-pressure intensity where you could barely dribble. If I got past my defender, I could easily score or get fouled. It took me the entire game to get adjusted to this, but when I noticed how easy it was for me to score, I liked it.

At the end of the game, I finished with about 15 points and 8 rebounds, but we lost. This was bad, because we only had one or two more games to make the playoffs. If we lost one, or both of them, the season would be over and I'd be heading back to America.

The next game we won, but I only had about 10 points, which was bad for me. Every game, I needed to score as much as possible so I could put it on my resume for the following season. In the final game before the playoffs, it was a road game and a must-win.

Finally adjusting to the style of play, I scored about 25 points, mixing in 3 pointers, free throws, and layups. I was in the zone and played extremely well. Unfortunately, not everybody else on our team did and we lost the game. Because of the loss, we didn't make the playoffs and the season ended.

I wasn't too invested in the team so I honestly didn't care that much. My initial goal in South America had been to play for a whole season, and I technically accomplished that. It wasn't pretty, but I did it. Over the next few days, the team directors paid us and sorted out our plane tickets. I asked if they could send me to New York but they said it was too expensive. My mom was living near Miami, so I asked if I could stay with her for a while. She agreed and the team booked me a ticket to Miami.

In my final few days in Valdivia, I explored the city. I ate lunch at the restaurant, watched the manatees, and took long walks along the river. At night I read, happy I didn't have to think about practice or winning basketball games anymore. I liked to play but the season had taken a lot out of me.

10
BACK TO AMERICA

When the wheels of the plane finally touched down in America, I exhaled a sigh of relief. Walking through customs, the security guard checked out my passport and, in a no-nonsense tone, asked, "What was the reason for your visit?"

"I was playing professional basketball."

His eyes lit up and he started asking me questions with genuine curiosity. I told him I attended Rowan University and he knew a few people who went there. We kept talking until he realized he was holding up the line and sent me on my way, wishing me well. I smiled as I thought, *What a great welcome back to America.*

My mom was excited to see me and gave me a big hug. The plan was to stay at her place for a while, figuring out if I wanted to move back to New York or try my hand at jobs in Pompano Beach. Since I got some stats from the season, I'd work over the summer then try to get onto a different team when the season started in the fall. Until then I'd try to stay in shape.

The drive to Pompano Beach from the Miami airport was peaceful. Palm trees lined the road, similar to Argentina, and the air was a cool seventy degrees. Her apartment was right at the edge of the ocean so I put on some sandals and walked to the beach. I looked up at the stars, thankful to be back in America.

--

I woke up the following day and saw how beautiful the area actually was. It was right on the beach and palm trees rested at the edge of the sand, as the coastline stretched on for miles. This was, in a word, paradise. Mar Del Plata was nice, but this was even better.

My goal for the first day was to find a gym and some basketball courts. Checking online, I found a gym nearby for only ten dollars per month with quality workout equipment. I then mapped out a few basketball courts.

Now I just needed a job.

The plan was to stay for the summer and then get on a team somewhere in the fall. So I didn't want to apply for a career job that would require I stay around. Something temporary would be perfect.

I applied online for a few bouncer jobs in Fort Lauderdale and got a few interviews. I didn't have a car, so I took the bus into the heart of the city, about thirty minutes away. Within the first week I got a job at a place downtown. The hours were 8 PM to 4 AM. However, after a few days I needed to find something better.

My mom's friend came to the apartment one day and suggested a place right on the beach in Fort Lauderdale called the Elbo Room. I asked if I should apply online and she just laughed at me, telling me they didn't have a working phone or internet. The only way to talk with them was going down there in person.

I went down the next morning and talked to the bartender. The place was right on the water and had been there since 1948. The bartender told me to come down the following day and speak with Jon, the hiring manager.

I showed up the next day dressed nicely, with my resume. Jon introduced himself and I got a sense he had been through his share of fights. Stocky and muscular, standing about 5'11" tall, he had a goatee and shaved head. Looking into his eyes, I could tell he meant business, and wanted someone to join him who meant the same.

He asked a few standard interview questions and I told him I worked as a bouncer in Philadelphia. I left out the part about it being a gay bar. He quizzed me a few more times about what to do in certain situations then put my number into his phone. He said that yes, they were hiring for the spring break season, so he'd let me know in a few days if I was on the schedule. Not wanting to push the matter, I thanked him and left.

For the next few days I continued to look for different jobs just in case, until I received a call from Jon. He asked if I still wanted the job. I said I did and he offered me forty hours a week, starting that night.

I took the bus there five days a week around 6 PM, then checked IDs and kept the peace at Elbo Room until 2 AM. Bus service stopped at 11 PM, so the only way to get back was to take a taxi or have my mom pick me up.

My mom was only working part time because she helped take care of my grandma nearby. The saying goes that a mother's love is the most powerful thing in the world, and that saying rings true when that mother drives thirty minutes at 2 AM every night to pick her son up from a bar.

After work one night, I was talking to a girl on the edge of the beach who I could tell liked me. At one point, she said, "I want to take you home with me."

A few seconds later, I heard a honk behind me. I looked up and it was my mom's car. I told the girl, "Sorry, but I have to go."

Looking surprised, she said, "What, is that your mom or something?"

"Actually… it is."

I gave her a kiss on the cheek, stood up, and walked over to the car, never to see her again.

--

Still expecting to play basketball in the fall, I worked out every day. Since I had to sleep late into the day it was a weird schedule but I got used to it.

I knew nobody in the area, so I went onto a dating website. There I met a girl named Danielle. We hit it off immediately and she was impressed with my experiences playing pro basketball. We began to spend a lot of time together, so when I wasn't playing basketball or working I hung out with her.

One day when I went to the outdoor basketball courts to work out, a father was playing with his son. When I finished my dribbling drills and sat down to rest the father walked over to me. "Hey man, I saw you working out and you're pretty good. You want to teach my son a few things?"

Looking over at his skinny, high school-aged son standing beneath the hoop, I replied, "Yea, sure."

We played one on one and he wasn't that bad. I obviously wasn't going to let him beat me but I didn't destroy him. I could tell he was surprised at how good I was, since there weren't too many pro basketball players in Pompano Beach. After the game I walked over to his dad to introduce myself. I told him I just came back from playing professionally overseas and was living in the area for the summer.

Surprised by this, he said, "Wow. Okay, he's trying out for the basketball team this coming year. Do you do training at all?"

"Yes, I do, actually." In reality I wasn't training anybody at the time, but I thought I knew enough to try it, especially with a high school kid.

"Okay great, how much do you charge?"

This one I had to think of on the fly, since I didn't have a price for my services yet. I wanted it to be cheap, but not too cheap. I responded, "Typically about thirty dollars a session."

He thought about it for a second then said, "Ok, take my information and Andrew's number and we can start training with you."

He looked over at his son, "Andrew, does that work for you?"

Replying in a quiet voice, Andrew said, "Yea, that's good."

I was excited to have another stream of income, but more importantly, someone to train with. Training gets lonely, and if you don't have someone else to hold you accountable it's hard to stay focused and motivated. Andrew became my training partner and we pushed each other along the way.

--

My strategy to get onto a team for the coming year wasn't really a strategy at all. It was more of a desperate hope. In August, I planned on reaching out to anybody I knew who was an agent or coach, hoping somebody would pick me up. Rick told me the odds of getting on a team were low, but I kept the hope alive anyway. What I *wasn't* going to do was fly to a random country and hustle to get on a team. Trying that two years in a row felt too risky, even for me.

To be honest, I was growing tired of the business of basketball. All I wanted was to play on a team for an entire season, then move up the ranks to the higher division, where I could play against better competition and make more money. I saw other guys I grew up with doing it, so why couldn't I? I didn't know what I was doing wrong and wondered why these teams didn't want me.

One day when I was walking to the gym behind a shopping plaza in the hot Florida sun, a thought entered my mind that forever changed my life. I thought, *Maybe it's* me. *Maybe I'm at fault. Maybe, instead of the teams being wrong, maybe I'm wrong.*

The reason this changed my life is because it planted the seed of ownership. Instead of blaming the players, teams, coaches, directors, cities, gyms, leagues, languages, or anything else, I put the blame on myself. When I treated it as *my* fault that I got kicked off those teams, that's when I realized I had a lot of improving to do. It was a turning point.

From that moment on, when I went to the library I didn't just check out thriller novels or Spanish books. I went to another section: Self-help. Even going into this section at first was uncomfortable because it proved that I wasn't perfect.

What I finally did was take accountability for my problems. In one book, an exercise told me to take an evaluation of my life, separating it into seven areas: Physical health, wealth, relationships, emotions, intelligence, self-growth, and spirituality. When I ranked myself from 1 to 10 in each area, I was disgusted by what I wrote down. Wealth? I was back living with my mom again and almost broke, so that definitely needed improvement. Emotions? I got angry too much, so I definitely needed to control that. Self-growth? I had no idea what that even meant. After the thorough evaluation, I realized that I had a lot of work to do.

On my free time, I read books about self-development. I read about emotional intelligence, controlling anger, and what it stemmed from. At one point I thought I needed a psychiatrist, but when I talked to one and she said it would cost $80 per session again, I thought, *Okay Tyson, how about you get a few books about your problems and create your own solutions? Diagnose and treat yourself, bro.*

I learned about meditation, motivation, habits, psychotherapy, and basically, why we do what we do. I tried to read two books a week on human development. At Elbo Room when it was slow, I'd read ebooks on my phone, learning everything I could about these topics.

One of the most interesting things I read was from Daniel Goleman's Emotional Intelligence. He explained that in every situation, the experience goes through the emotional part of your brain (the amygdala) first, then it goes to the intellectual area (the neocortex). This is how our brains are wired. Thousands of years ago this saved our lives by giving us quicker reaction times, but today it often gets us into trouble. Coupling this with the dozens of other psychology books I read, life started to make more sense.

--

For a few months, I had a nice routine training with Andrew during the day then finishing the night at Elbo Room. When August came, about a month before teams started picking players for their teams, I met a guy at work.

He was about 6'3" tall and strong, so as he walked past me I said, "Hey man, do you play football?"

He said, "Nah man, I play basketball. I'm trying to get on a team overseas somewhere."

Shocked, I said, "No way man, me too." We exchanged numbers and agreed to help each other get on a team somewhere in the fall.

We worked out together that weekend and he was a solid guard. His name was Jim and he had played at a small college nearby. He was 25 years old but hadn't played overseas anywhere yet so he didn't have any stats or video. In our discussions on how to get on a team, he told me about an overseas tryout in Venice Beach, California. He said lots of scouts would be there and gave me the number for the guy who ran the tournament.

One night I called the guy in California, whose name was Dan. He gave me the details of the camp, such as who would be there and how much it would cost. Talking to him put my worries at ease since he seemed nice and the camp was only $50.

At this point, I felt like I was running out of options. The agents I reached out to didn't reply with positive news, many of them not responding at all. This camp in Venice Beach started to feel like my only hope. I trained all summer, so I hoped it would work out.

In late August, I took the weekend off from Elbo Room to fly out to Los Angeles with Jim. When we got to the airport, we hadn't booked a hotel yet so we took a taxi to Venice Beach then found a cheap hotel near the gym. Jim also had another friend who was trying to get onto a team, so it was the three of us in a dingy room with two beds. I was taller than both of them so they let me have a bed to myself while they slept in the same bed together.

When the camp officially started, there were some good players… but no scouts. The first night was just drills, and then they put us on teams for the rest of the weekend. I started to worry that it seemed sketchy but wanted to be positive and give it the benefit of the doubt.

The next day when I showed up at game time, Dan, the agent who I spoke with on the phone, was nowhere to be seen. We waited in the gym for three hours, watching other people play until Dan finally showed up. Inquiring about what happened, he said the times got changed. I thought, *Well why the hell didn't you tell us?*

We waited another hour until we finally got to play. But by then everybody had already left the gym. There were no scouts and maybe one agent was standing in the corner next to a family. I played well in the game but it didn't matter because nobody was there to see it. That night I ate alone at a McDonald's, since that was the only place open. By then I thought the trip was bullshit.

On the final day, we heard that someone from the previous day had gotten a deal to play in Mexico for $10,000 a month. I didn't know if it was true or not since I hadn't seen any scouts. I found out later that the rumor was completely false.

Before our last game at 6 PM we all hung out on Venice Beach. As the sun set on the outside courts, I just wanted to play pickup ball. My intuition told me the games that night would be a waste of time, but I went anyway since I had made a commitment. When we got to the gym, barely anybody was there. No agents, scouts, or anybody who could help me get on a team in a foreign country. I hit a few shots and we lost the game, but it didn't matter. It was a wasted trip.

A few days after I got back to Florida, Dan called me again.

"Tyson, you played great at the camp in Venice and I think you really have a shot to get on a team. There's a camp I know of in Atlanta where there will be lots of scouts, and teams need shooters like you."

Extremely skeptical, I got to the bottom of the matter, "Thanks, Dan. How much is it?"

"It's $300, but if you get on a team it'll be worth it."

Rolling my eyes, I played his game. "Okay, and I'd have to fly myself there?"

"Yes."

Acting like the innocent player with dreams of the NBA, I said, "Okay, well is there any way you could help out with the payment? That's a little expensive, plus I'll be paying for my own plane ticket."

"Oh man, I would, but my money's all tied up right now. I'd love to but I can't. You're a great shooter though, and you should definitely go."

"Okay, well let me think about it. I'll get back to you in the next few days."

"Great, man. Let's talk soon."

Some people try to sell the dream. But it takes more than $300 for a two-day camp for a childhood dream of making the NBA to come true.

If 100 people pay $300 for a camp, that's $30,000 going into the pockets of whoever created it. Guys like Dan no doubt get a commission for getting athletes to attend. Maybe they hire a few scouts to come to make it seem like there's representation, but from what I could tell a lot of it seemed for show. The hard truth is that if you're not on the radar of scouts before one of these camps, the odds of making a name for yourself there are extremely low.

When Dan called back a few days later to ask if I was interested in going to the camp in Atlanta, I texted back that I couldn't make it. I figured he probably moved on to other athletes with dreams of NBA riches and stardom.

--

August turned into September and the reality hit that I most likely wasn't going to get on a team. I wanted to play but I wasn't going to fly to a random country hoping to somehow get picked. It worked in Argentina, but I didn't want to try it again.

Still working at the Elbo Room, something happened one night that gave me direction. I was off when I got a text from a co-worker saying that Christian, another co-worker, had been shot. I thought the guy was messing around but I gave him a call. He said he wasn't lying; Christian had been shot and was in the hospital.

Asking around, I figured out what happened. Christian, one of the nicest guys I'd ever met and the one who instructed me on my first day, had escorted a drunk guy out of the bar. On the way out, the guy tripped over him and they fell to the ground. The guy thought Christian was trying to take him down, so he pulled out a gun and shot him in the stomach. Christian was alive, but in the ICU and needed major surgery to save his life.

Once we all found out about this, it shook up the whole staff. Nobody wanted to get shot on this job, especially since there were no benefits and we were only getting paid slightly higher than minimum wage. Breaking up a fight was one thing, but getting shot just doing your job? That's not what we signed up for. A few guys quit and I realized I needed to find something else, too. The scariest part for me was that Christian had been working the part of the bar I usually covered. If I had been on that night it could have easily been me getting shot.

So I applied for dozens of different jobs. There was an opening for a sales rep at a car dealership down the street, and with my experience in sales I thought it'd be perfect. I thought, *I can sell cars.*

For my interview, the manager told me to sell him a pen. I sold the shit out of that pen and started working there the next week. It was ironic that I sold cars since I didn't own one and rode my bike to work every day.

Selling cars came with a huge learning curve but I slowly learned. My manager trained us on the path to sales, which included understanding the customer's needs, showing them the product, then negotiating price.

I learned a lot, but over time, I began to see why used car salesmen are the least-trusted people on the planet. Shady things went down that I could have never believed. Guys smiled at each other then stabbed each other in the back. Details were omitted from contracts while numbers got inflated. When a new potential customer pulled in, guys swarmed like vultures, hoping to shake that person's hand and solidify them as their client. I even had a guy physically push me out of the way for a customer. The whole thing seemed like the twilight zone.

One time I overheard a customer talking about handwriting analysis. It caught my attention because I had just been reading about it. When I brought it up to him, he sat me down and analyzed my handwriting. From one short sample, he gave me an analysis of my life. He said he could determine a person's IQ through their handwriting. Skeptical, I went along with his game. He asked a few questions, counted on his fingers, and said, "You have an IQ of 180."

Looking it up, I saw that a 180 IQ is genius level. He told me that if I really started to put my brain to use, I wouldn't be working at this little car dealership. The IQ thing may not have been real, but it still gave me confidence that there was more out there for me.

--

Thinking about what I could do other than selling cars, I started to get ideas for businesses. Diving into entrepreneurship articles online, it seemed like a common theme was to follow your passion. Mine was obvious: Basketball.

I started to figure out how I could create a business with it. Personal training had its place, but I could only train a certain number of people every week. The internet, I thought, was much easier. I checked out different e-commerce basketball websites and determined how much they would make if a certain number of people bought their product. I figured that if I made three different package levels, with 10,000 people buying a package, I could make a million dollars pretty quickly. I figured I'd do almost anything to get out of the car dealership, so I started to put it together.

Telling my dad about the idea, he put me in touch with someone to help create the website. Creating a professional website was expensive, so my dad and grandma invested some money into it. All the time that I spent away from the dealership I put into the website. I created training ebooks, in which a user could just click the link and be taken to the drill they wanted to do. Not holding anything back, I made sections for shooting, ball handling, defense, vertical jump, stretching, rebounding, passing, strength training, and information on the mental, emotional, and political sides of basketball.

At the same time, the busy season of Fort Lauderdale was approaching, so I applied to work as a bar back at a restaurant along the beach. I had heard stories of bar backs making over $500 per night and I wanted a piece of that action. Plus, the place was right on the beach.

The job was doing dirty work like cleaning tables, refilling the ice bin, making margaritas, taking the trash out, and anything else that needed to be done. That was fine with me, so on the week before New Year's I ended my stint selling cars.

When I started at the bar I was put on the day shift during the middle of the week. The busy times were nights and weekends, which I was hoping for, but the manager said the other guys had been there longer so they deserved the prime shifts. I was discouraged but hoped I'd still make some good money.

In my off hours, I trained with Andrew and focused on the website. Andrew wasn't getting much playing time on his school team and eventually quit because of politics, similar to what I had experienced at Maine. However, he became an All-State athlete in pole vault, so I like to think that all our training wasn't in vain.

For the website I eventually created over 400 videos, and in the process I learned a lot about how to start a business. I hoped that on launch day the money would start to roll in, but until that day I wanted everything to be perfect.

As the busy season got into swing in Fort Lauderdale, I wasn't making nearly as much as I thought I would. The days were slow. One day when I arrived before my shift, I saw a guy lazily smoking a cigarette about to go into work at the bar next door. I thought, *Tyson, are you serious? You can do better than this.*

I never experienced the $500 nights I had hoped for. After Spring Break ended, the manager told me my hours were going to be shortened. There was nothing I could say, so I agreed. Then one night at my girlfriend Danielle's apartment, I checked the schedule to see what my hours were for that week. I didn't see any times so I refreshed the page. My name wasn't anywhere.

I called the manager and he confirmed that they didn't need me anymore. But he said, "If you need a reference for any other job, put my name down and I'll give you one."

I had saved up some money so I didn't freak out, but it wasn't a good feeling being let go from another job. I tried to figure out what my next steps were.

In July, the basketball website officially went live. I was expecting thousands of views with dozens of orders every day. I mean, these were quality basketball workouts with a professional website. Who *wouldn't* pay $97 for a package?

After the first two days, nobody bought anything. I kept up hope, realizing it was only the beginning. Two days later there were no purchases, and a week later, still nothing. I thought I'd get about 1,000 views per day, but it was more like 10.

Over the next two months, the only people who bought training programs were my mom and my dad, probably feeling pity for me about my first business. Every day I tweaked the site, created blogs, and reached out to people who I thought would like it, but nothing helped. Two years later, not many people have purchased a package and the site doesn't get much traffic.

At the end of the summer, my girlfriend Danielle said she was moving to Texas for college. We'd been together for over a year and had a solid relationship, but when she said she was moving it annoyed me. She didn't talk with me about it, she just said it matter-of-factly. I could have left for New York at any point, but a big reason why I stayed in Florida was for her.

Even though I was annoyed, she asked if I could drive her car with her belongings to Texas. Wanting to be a supportive boyfriend, I agreed. On the day of my trip, I said bye to my mom, telling her I'd be back at some point. I didn't know if my life would continue in Texas or somewhere else, but without a job in Florida I was ready for a change.

When we got to Texas, I stayed with her for a few weeks until I realized it wasn't going to work out. There were no jobs and I didn't even have a car. Praying on what I should do next, I called my aunt in New York City. She said if I needed to stay at her place for a while I could, and it seemed like a great idea. It'd be new opportunities and new people. With my knowledge and skills, I had confidence I could get a job there pretty quickly. Danielle didn't want to see me leave, but we both agreed that New York was the best option.

--

I bought a one-way ticket to New York City and when I got there, applied to about fifty jobs a day. Danielle was actually now excited that I lived in New York so she could visit when she had a chance. After two weeks of hustling and interviews, I got a job selling advertising space at a tech company. They provided me with a salary, benefits, and stock options, things I'd never had before. I was extremely grateful for the chance.

Going back to New York felt like a rebirth. Florida was nice but the pace was slow and there wasn't much of a basketball scene. Since I didn't have a car there, unlike most people, it was hard to get to know anybody.

On one of my first days back in New York, I got an email from Bobbito about an open run workout. I hadn't played in one of those in years, so I was excited to play again. When everybody showed up, it was like nothing had changed.

Bobbito said to me, "Tyson, didn't I light you up on this court once before?"

I was surprised Bobbito remembered this because he had spent the past two years traveling around the world promoting his documentary, meeting thousands of people along the way. Before he left we had played two on two on the same court. I had guarded Bobbito and on a few plays, I gave him too much space and he hit a few jumpers. I remembered it vividly but didn't think someone with his celebrity status would.

Laughing at the fact that he brought it up, I had to reply, "Yes... yes you did."

The thing about basketball is that classy players won't talk trash. Classy players won't rub it in your face if they score five straight points on you. But what they will do is remember it. They'll remember every detail and store it in their memory bank, so if push comes to shove, they can bring it up. Or, two years later, they can drop a subtle comment reminding you about it.

Fall turned into winter and outdoor basketball wasn't a possibility anymore. However, a friend from New Jersey was living in New York and got me into a basketball league downtown. Games were once a week and it was some of the best competition in the city. Many players on the opposing teams played overseas, with a few who had even played in the NBA. Still having talent, I averaged about 20 points per game in that league.

I was still with Danielle, and she came to visit once but wanted me to pay for everything. I was getting a decent salary but told her the tickets were still too expensive for me to pay for it all. The distance was getting too hard for us, and on Valentine's Day we ended our relationship.

In a routine at work, I performed my sales position forty hours per week, while trying to play as much basketball as I could on the weekend. My main goal at the job was to stay there at least a year, since my resume was dotted with three months here, six months there. Employers don't like to see that, just as professional teams overseas don't like to see that. The goal was to make my resume look good.

When it got warmer outside, I started to play streetball again…and it was heaven. The streetball scene in New York City is unlike anywhere else in the world. On a warm, sunny day, you can find games at any outdoor court. On the major holidays and weekends, when most people were drinking or relaxing at the beach, I played at courts all over the city until it got dark.

When summer approached, Bobbito's Full Court 21™ tournament started again. I wasn't able to play in it the previous summer since I was in Florida, but this year I was determined to win. It was his concept and it works like this: There's about five players on the court together and every player works for themselves. The game is up to 21 points. If you make a shot you get two points, then you are allowed a maximum of three shots from the top of the free throw area, which are worth one point each. When you miss one of these shots, the ball is in play again.

That's a classic game of 21, except Bobbito's twist was that it was played on a full court. Typically 21 is played only on a half-court, because full court is extremely tiring. If the ball changes possession, the person with the ball has to dribble the length of the court, trying to score at the opposite hoop. All the while, you've got three or four people playing defense on you, trying to steal the ball.

In the beginning of the summer, my only goal was to win that tournament.

Not taking any chances, I trained incessantly. I did sprints and shot for hours on Saturday mornings. I thought of a strategy and made sure that even if I wasn't the best, I'd be in the best shape. There were weekly qualifiers to make it into the championship game at the end of the summer. Qualifying in one of the first weeks, I locked in my spot for the championship game.

The day of the championship came and I rushed home from work to give myself adequate time to warmup. Honestly, I didn't think I would win, despite my training. I was 6'6" and playing against smaller guys who were much quicker. That gave me a disadvantage because they could easily steal the ball. However, my height gave me an advantage for rebounds.

A few of my family members attended the game and it was livestreamed over the internet. The court was at the edge of Harlem and a crowd circled the pavement in front of a chain-link fence, making it feel like the videos I had seen growing up of the legendary streetball court Rucker Park. Graffiti plastered the walls and cracks dotted the pavement, so if a player didn't have good handle they could easily lose the ball.

In the first half, I did a spin move on offense that made a defender fall. The crowd cheered. I got my nerves out and got into the flow of the game. When the second half started, the leading scorer had twelve points while I only had five. I thought there was no chance I would win and was happy to at least have a highlight in the first half. I kept playing, however, hoping I'd find an opening.

With two minutes left in the game, I was still down seven points. In theory, that could be made up pretty quickly with two baskets and three free throws, but that's hard to do.

On one play, I stole the ball and made a layup. I made only one shot though, which put me down four points. Then, with twenty seconds left to go, I stole the ball again and made another shot. Now, I only needed to make two free throws to tie, three to win. The clock was against me as the announcer counted it down.

"Ten... nine... eight..."

I made my first free throw.

"Five… four… three… two…"

I made my second.

The score was tied at twelve as the clock ran down to zero. In the case of a tie there's an old-fashioned shoot out. One person shoots an NBA three pointer. If they make it and the other misses, the person who makes it wins. If they both make it, they keep shooting.

The sun had set long ago and the moon and stars had appeared in the night sky. The crowd circled around the half-court as Bobbito announced the rules. When he got done, he said, "Okay Tyson, you shoot first."

The irony about this moment is that in the first week of the summer, I lost in a similar shootout to the same player. This guy was a quick guard, about 6' tall, who played at a Division 2 college. In the first week, he had made his shot but I missed mine. Now, I had a chance for redemption.

I walked up to Bobbito and grabbed the ball. I took a deep breath. This was the hoop I had been training at all summer. I took a dribble, stepped up to the three point line, and shot.

SWISH.

Pumped up, I walked away from the spot, knowing that if he made ten straight shots I'd beat him on the eleventh. As Woody Harrelson said from *White Men Can't Jump*, I was in the zone.

The crowd cheered and waited in anticipation for my rival to shoot.

He took the ball, shot it, and it bounced off the rim.

I was the 2014 Full Court 21™ Champion.

I shook hands with people and they congratulated me for a few minutes. When the celebration died down I interviewed with a few members of the press, including SLAM Magazine. I'd been wanting to get into SLAM since high school, and I was now getting my chance, ten years later and on the streets of New York City.

For winning the tournament, I received a pair of new shoes and a few other prizes. But most importantly, I got the one thing I always wanted: An authentic streetball nickname. Guys gave me nicknames all the time on the courts, but receiving one from a legend like Bobbito Garcia was the real deal. Because I played with him all summer and he liked making up names for me, he gave me three. Top Gun, Tom Cruise and Clark Gable.

Walking back to my apartment after everybody left, I felt so empowered. Yes, I was working a full-time job, but basketball was in my fucking soul. I felt deep in my bones that it was what I was on this earth to do. Winning this championship just solidified that fact. I could go away from basketball for as long as I wanted, but like it always has throughout my life, it will always pull me back in.

EPILOGUE

When I'm on the basketball court, I feel freedom…I feel life…I feel love. At times it's gotten too much for me but that's when I slow down. Circumstances may have ruined my love for the game temporarily in the past, but I knew deep down that eventually I'd be back. Ideally I'd be playing basketball every day, not having to worry about money or anything else, but that didn't end up being my story.

Just a year ago, I would have never written any of this. I was scared to tell people I got kicked off my teams, much less what happened between my sophomore and junior years of college. But basketball has kept creeping its way back into my life. God wanted me to tell this story and I believe He chose me for a reason.

Honestly, I was nervous writing this. Most people don't offer up their lives on a platter. They keep things deep inside so nobody knows what happened. They don't want to be seen as weird, ugly, or not fitting in.

But me? I'm okay with being different. Doing what's not normal is normal to me, so that's why I'm okay with writing this. And I feel like I was put through many of these things not for me, but for you.

Maybe by reading this you will feel a renewed sense of spirit for your life. Maybe you'll take the first step toward achieving what you've always wanted. Maybe you will make amends to people from your past or pay attention to things you missed before. Or, maybe to you this is just an interesting story about a kid who got too sucked into basketball.

Recently, a family member told me she had worried that I was too into basketball when I was younger. Reading this story, it's easy to believe that. But then I thought, *What if the opposite is true?* Maybe I *wasn't* as dedicated as

I could have been. Maybe I could have learned more, done more, and been deeper involved in the game. Would that have made my life better? Or would these things have happened to me regardless of how hard I worked?

In the end, I don't think there's an answer to that. I can't second-guess my actions. Would I go back and change things if possible? Of course. I don't have that luxury though. I can't go back and change scenarios or bring my friends back to life. I do wonder why they're gone, though, and why I'm still here. What makes me so special?

Is life about working hard and then succeeding at what you want to accomplish? Is it about writing down your goals and then achieving them? If I became a star athlete in college then made the NBA, would I have written a book like this? Maybe, but would the story be as compelling? Probably not. A guy achieves his goals…that's great.

Maybe life isn't about our successes, then. Maybe it's about the opposite. Maybe it's about our failures. Maybe it's about our shortcomings, our flaws, and our ugliness. Maybe it's about working our ass off for something, not getting it, getting depressed and discouraged, but instead of letting that depression take over, we get back up. We feel a renewed sense of spirit, knowing the next time we want to accomplish something, we're going to prepare even harder, focus even more, and leave absolutely no chance for failure.

It's about the universal things we all experience day by day, but are scared to act on. It's about the book you're scared to write. It's about the business you're afraid to start. It's about the school basketball team you're scared to try out for, but you try out anyway. Then when you get kicked out of practice, it just fuels your fire to play even harder instead of getting discouraged. It's about that person in your life who you have a bad relationship with, but you reach out to them with love regardless, knowing they won't be around forever. It's about being nice to the nerd in your class, seeing that just because they don't sit with anybody at the lunch table doesn't mean they're a loser.

Maybe that kid's not a loser at all. Maybe that kid's much cooler than you, he just hasn't hit his stride in life yet. And maybe in six months you'll drop off and be where he is. Life is perpetual, and the only thing we can control is how we act day by day.

Are we going to be good to others or treat them badly? Are we going to show up on time or late? Are we going to put the extra work in or only do the minimum? Are we going to bring people down around us or uplift them, knowing and believing they can do more?

A fact of my life is that when I worked hard, good things happened. I couldn't control everything, but when I truly, honestly worked hard, things somehow worked out. When I didn't work hard, like in my senior year of college when I drank all the time and got lazy, I racked up legal fees and got into trouble. But when I shot outside in the cold for hours every single night during my freshman year of high school, what happened? I played Varsity the next season. It's not rocket science. Hard, honest work makes good things happen.

I think that's the most interesting fact about life. There are no shortcuts. The world today is telling you to drink a smoothie and you'll have the perfect body. Download an ebook and you'll make six figures. Buy a workout program and you'll make the NBA. It seems that everybody wants, and thinks they can get, anything in less than a week.

The reality is the opposite. I wish I had a tracker of how many shots I took over my life or how many hours I put into the gym. I could take this number to the kids I train and say, "This is what it takes, so be prepared."

Steven Pressfield, bestselling author of *The War of Art*, wrote, "We're not born with unlimited choices. We can't be anything we want to be. We come into this world with a specific, personal destiny. We have a job to do, a calling to enact.

"If tomorrow morning by some stroke of magic every dazed and benighted soul woke up with the power to take the first step toward pursuing his or her dreams, every shrink in the directory would be out of business. Prisons would stand empty. The alcohol and tobacco industries would collapse, along with the junk food, cosmetic surgery, and infotainment businesses, not to mention pharmaceutical companies, hospitals, and the medical profession from top to bottom."

That's a bold statement but I see where he's coming from. He means that if you're pursuing what you really want in this world, there's no need for the extra bullshit. There's no need to watch six hours of TV if you know you could be spending it on training, creating a business, or pursuing your craft. If you have visions for what your life looks like outside of your immediate situation, it will keep lighting the fire inside to become what you want to become, no matter your circumstance.

We all have a calling to fulfill. Mine was basketball. Get in touch with yours and take the first steps toward who you were meant to become.

Word.

--

ABOUT THE AUTHOR

Tyson Hartnett was an All-American in high school, played basketball at the Division 1 and 3 levels, and played professionally in three different countries. He currently contributes to the Huffington Post, Elite Daily, and Esquire Network, and has been featured in SLAM Magazine. Today, he helps athletes through many common struggles throughout their careers. He created a website with basketball training drills, BasketballTrainingClub.com, and also runs an online support group for athletes called The Athlete's Corner. You can contact him at Tyson.Hartnett@gmail.com.

Made in the USA
San Bernardino, CA
17 November 2015